NEW MEXICO COLCHA CLUB

I0891932

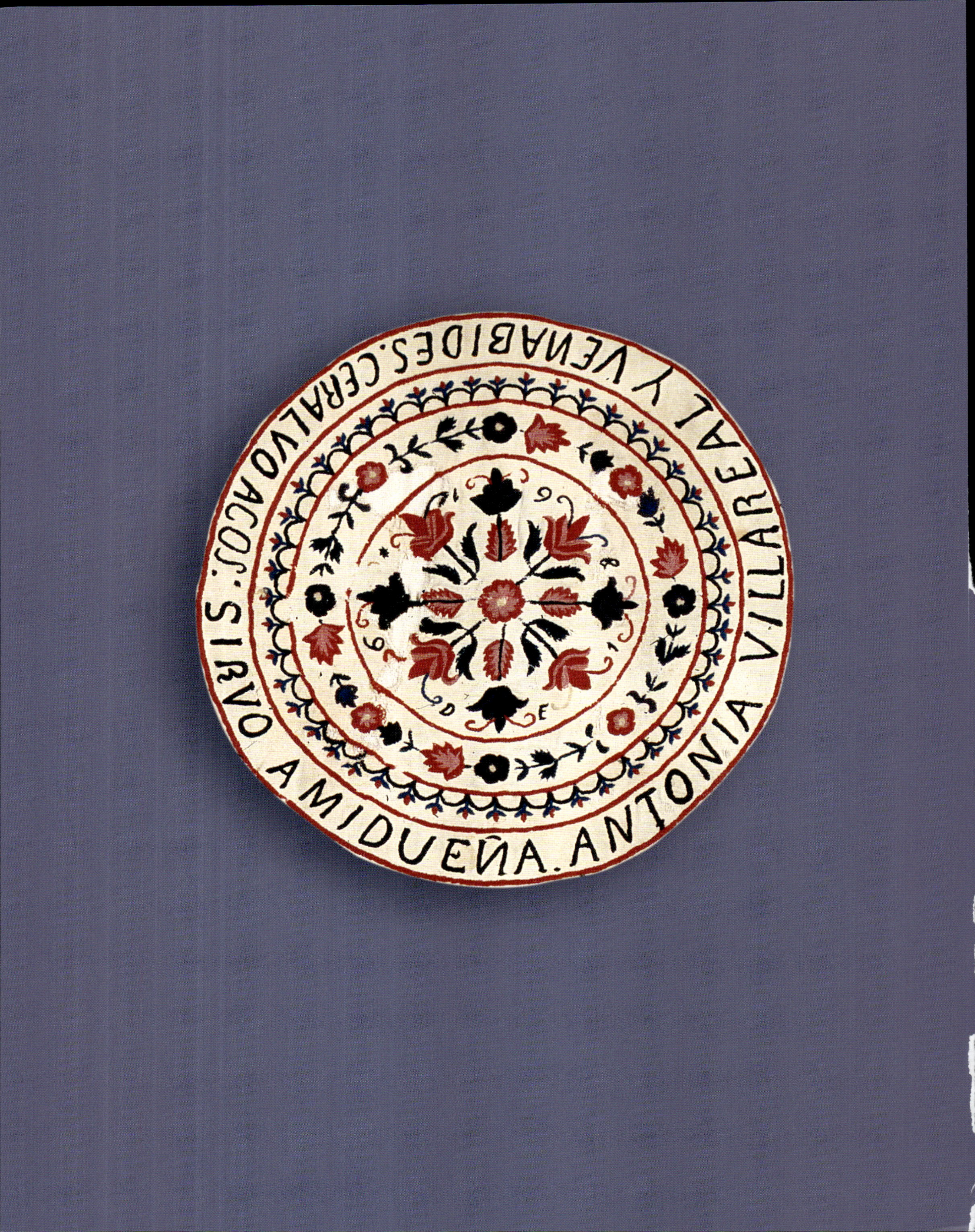
SIRVO A MIDUEÑA. ANTONIA VILLAREAL Y VENABIDES. CERALVO ACOS:

NEW MEXICO COLCHA CLUB

SPANISH COLONIAL EMBROIDERY & THE WOMEN WHO SAVED IT

Nancy C. Benson

MUSEUM OF NEW MEXICO PRESS
SANTA FE

In memory of Mary Reynolds

(1945–2007)

A loving friend who showed us how to go forth
and enjoy life

 Museum of New Mexico Press is a division of New Mexico Department of Cultural Affairs.

Project director: Mary Wachs
Design and production: Bette Brodsky
Map by Deborah Reade
Composition: Set in Brioso Pro
Manufactured in China
10 9 8 7 6 5 4 3 2 1

ISBN 978-089013-519-8

Museum of New Mexico Press
Post Office Box 2087
Santa Fe, New Mexico 87504
www.mnmpress.org

Page 2: Detail (see page 78). Embroidered bedspread, Mexico, mid-nineteenth century. Courtesy Museum of Spanish Colonial Art, Collections of the Spanish Colonial Arts Society, Inc., Santa Fe (1980.1).

CONTENTS

ACKNOWLEDGMENTS

My friend Esther Lujan Vigil was the catalyst for this book, as well as the primary source of information. Over the past four years, Esther has written her memories of life in the Española Valley, explored her genealogy, ferreted out facts and talked with past acquaintances, shared her convictions about colcha embroidery, and corralled a compelling collection of old family photos. My sincere thanks to Esther, Joe, and their wonderful children Jeanette, Danny, Victor, and Stella for making this project possible.

I am equally indebted to Josie Caruso, the independent scholar and textile restorer who vetted the book proposal and part 1 of the manuscript. Her passion for the textiles and history of New Mexico has enriched the text immeasurably. We share a love of books, but Josie wisely understood that I could not write convincingly about colcha embroidery unless I examined the real thing. The mornings I spent with her unwrapping, discussing, and rewrapping all the colchas in the Museum of Spanish Colonial Art were as fruitful as they were fun.

My gratitude goes to the many friends and acquaintances who contributed to the research effort. Tillie Gonzales, Aurelia Madrid, and Libby Cata Marquez graciously provided a wealth of information about Teofila and the Arte Antiguo. Fred Vigil shared his memories of Teofila as a teacher and homemaker. Ree Mobley at the Bartlett Library of the Museum of International Folk Art in Santa Fe deftly produced hard-to-find books and

Opposite: Eight members at a meeting of the Arte Antiguo in 1954. Seated (left to right): Rosa Rodriguez, Eloisa Maestas, and Flora Roybal. Standing (left to right): Mrs. Americo Romero, Teofila Lujan, Syria Lucero, Josie Delgado, and Aggie Serna. Courtesy of Esther Vigil.

journal articles. Rita Padilla Haufmann heightened my understanding of the history of weaving in New Mexico, as well as the process of preparing a fleece, then spinning, dyeing, and weaving the yarn.

Robin Farwell Gavin, curator at the Museum of Spanish Colonial Art, has provided invaluable support since the inception of the book. First she pointed me to Josie. Thereafter, she was quick to respond to my requests for reference works, sources of information, and appropriate images. Robin is living proof of the maxim that those who have the most to do are the most productive. I am also grateful to Robin's assistant curator Alessa Greenway Palacio for her kind words and deft camera work.

Kathleen McClellan, a voracious reader, directed me to several museum exhibition publications that contain valuable sources I would have found nowhere else. I thank my long-term friend for the boundless encouragement she has given me.

I am also indebted to many others for the help they provided during my research efforts: Dorothy Amsden in Los Alamos; Loretta Atencio at the San Gabriel Museum in Española; Michaele Haynes, curator at the Witte Museum in San Antonio; Susan Poorbaugh, librarian at the New Mexico Museum of Art in Santa Fe; Kathleen Gavey at the Menaul Historical Library of the Southwest in Albuquerque; Deb Slaney, curator of history at the Albuquerque Museum of Art and History; Bobbie Sumberg, curator of textiles at the Museum of International Folk Art; Bunny Huffman, director of operations at the Acequia Madre House in Santa Fe; Al Regensberg, senior archivist at the New Mexico Records Center and Archives; and Judy Dewey, Santa Fe collector and gallery owner.

I extend my thanks again to the staff of all the museums, institutions, and collections who helped me acquire illustrations for this book. Two young museum professionals were especially adroit in responding to my request for photographs of textiles in their collections: Saskia Kesners at the Colorado Springs Fine Arts Center Taylor Museum and Lila Scott at the Acequia Madre House in Santa Fe. My sincere wishes for continued success to both of you.

At a workshop many years ago, I fell into a long conversation with a technical communicator who is equally talented as a writer and illustrator. We've been enjoying one another's company ever since. I'm grateful to the indomitable Doris Parry for creating our diagram of the colcha stitch.

Two photographers provided highly capable and indispensable support for this effort. Tony Reynolds and Dr. Dan Richey captured images that testify dramatically to the skill and imagination of New Mexico's colcha embroiderers. Tony spent many hours in his studio documenting examples of the colcha art created by Esther Lujan. His art school training and enthusiasm for Esther's embroidery surely contributed to the success of his efforts. Dan exercised his innate sense of design and considerable technical prowess to capture the beauty of the historic and contemporary colchas that others graciously provided. I'm indebted to both my good friends for their generosity, commitment, and hard work.

Had editorial director Mary Wachs not shared my enthusiasm for developing a book on colcha embroidery, I would never have had the privilege of working with her and her talented associates at the Museum of New Mexico Press. I admire Mary's cheerful professionalism and the body of work she manages to produce. Her recommendations and guidance on this project have been invaluable.

The aspect of this project I cherish most is the role played by family members. My daughter Jennifer Bown, a talented technical writer and editor, nailed the awkward sentences and mixed metaphors in my book proposal. She reviewed the manuscript with the same loving, but lethal, editorial eye. I couldn't be more proud of her.

Last in the credits — and first in my heart — is my patient and devoted husband, Dave. He has been my sounding board, photo archivist, critical reader, computer consultant, and source of constant encouragement. Without his help, I could never have produced this book. *Merci mille fois, mon amour et ma vie.*

Detail of a colcha embroidery by Kathleen Sais-Lerner. The bedspread won Best of Show at Spanish Market in Santa Fe, New Mexico, in 2007. It measures 90.5 by 91.5 inches and is solidly embroidered in natural wool on muslin. Photo by Dave Benson.

PREFACE

Women in Spanish colonial New Mexico added beauty and warmth to their bedcovers by embroidering on them in a long couching stitch, creating the flowing needlework that today we call colcha embroidery. In Spanish, *colcha* means "bedspread" or "quilt."

This book is a biography of the Spanish colonial embroidery tradition in New Mexico. Readers will learn how the embroidery was born on the isolated and arid frontier, was nourished by loving hands, reached maturity, suffered a near-fatal decline, and was nursed back to health by two women of determination, passion, and creativity — Teofila Ortiz Lujan and her daughter Esther Lujan Vigil.

Like the settlers who journeyed fifteen hundred miles north from Mexico City in 1598 to put down roots in the remote province of New Mexico, Teofila was an adventurous, spirited individual who embraced change while remaining true to the traditions of her culture. Esther has followed in her mother's footsteps. Their story provides a window to the past — to the strong, independent women who brought their customs and faith from the Old World to a harsh, unforgiving land and managed to endure the birth throes of the province.

In 1980 I drove up to Española and spent the day interviewing and photographing Teofila for an article that appeared in the Denver Post's *Empire Magazine*. She was eighty-five

Teofila Lujan, age eighty-five, at home in Española, New Mexico. Photo by Nancy C. Benson.

at the time, and I had a hard time keeping up with her. She was determined to show me everything—her embroidery, the farmhouse, the Santa Cruz church, the colchas in the homes of her old friends in the Arte Antiguo.

Decades before, Teofila had helped establish the Arte Antiguo, an organization of twelve Hispanic women dedicated to preserving colcha embroidery. It was clear that the club was important to her, but I failed to flesh out any details because she rushed off to find something else she wanted me to see.

Several years after Teofila died, Esther — my former neighbor in Albuquerque — got in touch with me. Expressing her deep concern that colcha would disappear and be forgotten now that her mother and the Arte Antiguo were gone, she asked me to help her keep the dying art alive for future generations.

Learning how the Arte Antiguo effected a local revival of the embroidery tradition was a logical way to begin, so we made several trips to Española and started asking questions. Answers were hard to find. Most of Teofila's contemporaries had died. One was in a nursing home and incapacitated. A daughter showed us several pieces of her mother's embroidery but couldn't recall how the club operated.

Discouraged by the lack of results, we were elated when the breakthrough came. Tillie Gonzalez, one of the club's last living members, welcomed us into her home, reminisced at length about the other members, and showed us examples of their embroidery. Then she left the room and returned with a box, which she offered to Esther for safekeeping. In the box were minutes of club meetings and the Arte Antiguo scrapbook — complete with newspaper clippings and photographs of the group over several decades.

Buoyed by the images and information in the scrapbook, Esther escalated her campaign to preserve colcha as art. She did demonstrations of the embroidery and taught classes. She produced a colcha embroidery instruction book and new patterns for her students. And she continued creating a body of work that brings new life to the ancient art by transcending traditional patterns and techniques. An innovative needle artist, she has achieved exciting new textures, color schemes, and compositions in her meticulously executed colcha embroidery.

In part 1 of this book, readers will discover the roots of the New Mexico embroidery tradition and learn why, when, and where the distinctive embroidery appears. They will watch it grow to maturity and then suffer a serious decline. Part 2 tells Teofila's story — the revival of colcha embroidery in the early years of the twentieth century. Part 3 offers Esther's story — the renaissance of colcha embroidery today and its transformation from folk art into fine art.

Details of the history of the embroidery in part 1 were drawn from the writings of such distinguished scholars of the material culture of colonial New Mexico as John Kessell, Marc Simmons, E. Boyd, Robin Gavin, José Esquibel, Myra Ellen Jenkins, Ward Alan Minge, and France Scholes. Based on these and additional sources, I identify and discuss the primary roots of colcha embroidery: the Spanish passion for embroidered textiles; hearty little churro sheep from Spain that sustained the colonists and provided the fleece that they made into the colcha ground fabric and embroidery yarn; designs from the Old World that migrated to northern New Mexico and appeared repeatedly in the region's distinctive embroidery.

In the published sources I also found intriguing facts about domestic life in colonial New Mexico. I took the liberty of building those facts into stories about the women who nurtured the needlework, produced colchas for export during the heyday of the embroidery, and developed a new branch of the embroidery midway through the nineteenth century.

Because of the efforts of many women over the past three centuries, the tradition of colcha embroidery is still alive today. The venerable embroidery will no doubt continue to evolve and develop new branches as it moves forward in time. I wish it a healthy and fruitful future.

Nancy C. Benson
Sandia Park, New Mexico

Fleece spun on a hand spindle. Photo by Dave Benson.

PART ONE

Roots of Colcha Embroidery in the Spanish Province of New Mexico

CHAPTER 1

1600s: The Difficult Birth of a Colony

The year was 1598, and the Globe Theatre was under construction on the south bank of the Thames. Shakespeare was completing *Hamlet*. In Spain, the king promised a lifetime pension to anyone who could discover a way to find the longitude at sea. In Italy, agents of the church threatened to execute heretics who asserted that the earth revolves around the sun. And John Alden, mythologized as the first pilgrim to set foot on Plymouth Rock, was born in England.

Juan de Oñate, a wealthy gentleman of New Spain, rode at the head of an advance party of soldier-settlers. They made camp at the Indian pueblo of Ohkay Owingeh and waited for the rest of the caravan to arrive. Oñate had chosen this spot on the banks of the Rio Grande — in what is today the high desert of the southwestern United States — to establish Spain's first colony in the province of New Mexico. An earlier explorer had reported that the Indians of this pueblo were friendly. Crops were plentiful, and the natives had offered no resistance to newcomers.

There, in the welcome shade of green cottonwood trees, the riders rested and refreshed themselves in the shallow river. A spectacular mountain range to the east promised mineral wealth and resources for the settlers. The new colony, sited an arduous fifteen hundred miles from Mexico City, would become the northernmost of Spain's holdings in the New World. It was also one of the places where the practice of colcha embroidery would emerge and flourish.

Opposite: Rear view of a jacket worn by a toreador. Photo by Alessa G. Palacio. Courtesy Museum of Spanish Colonial Art, Collections of the Spanish Colonial Arts Society, Inc., Santa Fe (2001.50c).

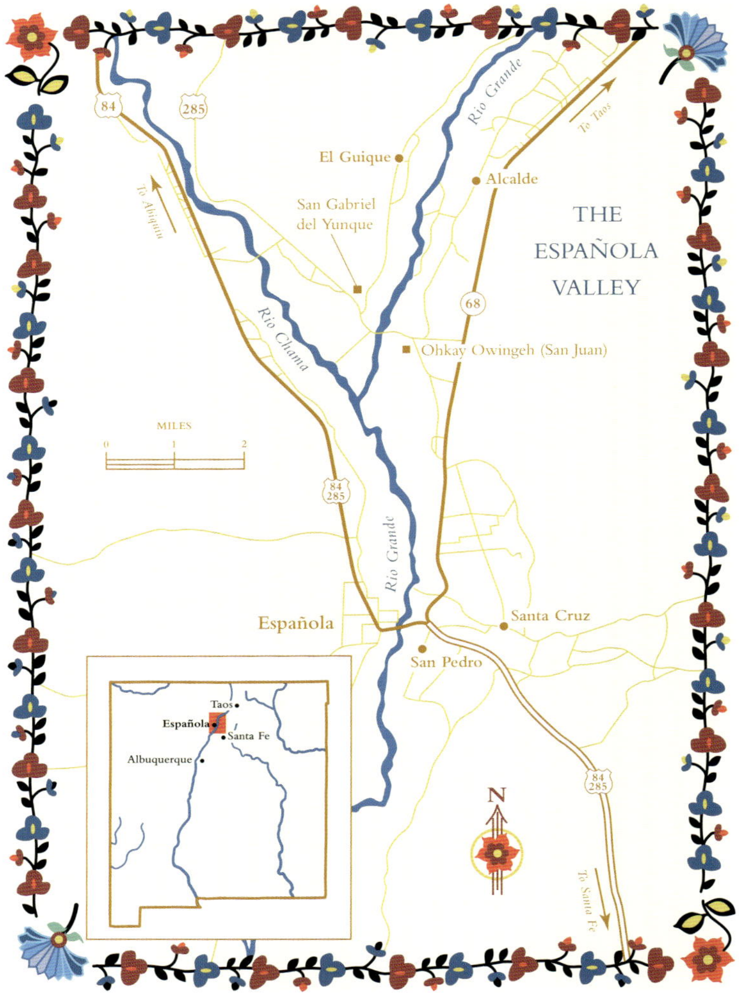

Map by DeborahReade

In 1598 Spain was well ahead of the other nations of Europe in conquering and settling the New World. The Spanish Crown's investment in the voyages of Christopher Columbus had paid off handsomely. Columbus had made four voyages to America between 1492 and 1502. Inspired by his accounts of strange and wonderful new lands filled with gold, Spaniards rushed to claim the riches. They established settlements in the Caribbean, then fanned out to explore the coast of Mexico. Adventurer Hernán Cortés led an expedition into the heartland of Mexico, defeated the native Aztec civilization in 1521, and, on the ruins of the Aztec capital, began construction of what was to become the capital of New Spain — Mexico City.

Adventurers continued to expand the rapidly growing colonial empire of Spain. By 1533 Francisco Pizarro had gained control of Peru and its native Inca civilization. Other Spaniards pushed forward to explore and colonize vast areas of land in Central and South America. By 1598 the empire of Spain stretched from the southernmost tip of South America to Oñate's settlement in New Mexico and included lands as far away as the Philippines.

The king of Spain maintained political and economic control of the far reaches of his empire by appointing regional viceroys to rule in his name. In 1595 Oñate received a contract from the viceroy of New Spain to outfit and transport an expedition to the province of New Mexico. The members of his expedition were to establish a permanent colony in the desolate lands on the far northern frontier of New Spain, a region that fellow Spaniard Francisco Vásquez de Coronado and others had explored half a century earlier.

Historian John Kessell paints a vivid picture of the teeming viceregal capital, Mexico City, in the mid-1590s, as recruiters vie to attract men and women to colonize one of three locations in Spain's expanding empire: New Mexico, California, and the Philippines. Sounding the fife and drum, the recruiters work hard to attract able colonists. The most desirable candidates are men and women who look fit and healthy, swear they are free of debt, and are willing to risk uncertainty for a new start in life (Kessell 2002:73).

With Oñate's appointment as first governor and captain general of the province of New Mexico came the authority to grant his recruits portions of the new land, the title of hidalgo (the lowest rank of Spanish nobility), and tribute from the native people. To be eligible for these rewards, however, the recruit had to remain on the land for five years. And anyone who abandoned the enterprise without official license was subject to death for desertion.

After a series of setbacks and delays, Oñate finally mustered his expedition at the departure point of Santa Bárbara, a mining town on the southern edge of the present-day Mexican state of Chihuahua. In late January 1598, they set out on the long trek north. His cavalcade of settlers trudging through the vast, arid lands of northern New Spain stretched

Scant Remains

In 1953 an official of Ohkay Owingeh Pueblo, digging in a field near the ruins of what had been Oñate's settlement, unearthed the bowl of a Spanish helmet—the earliest fragment of European armor ever found in the continental United States. Archaeologists excavating the site of San Gabriel in 1960 found fire pits, grinding stones, and Indian pottery made of micaceous clay in rooms that the Spanish had occupied. But little else remained that testified to the Spanish presence.

for several miles. It included hundreds of culturally Hispanic and racially mixed recruits, some with their Mexican Indian servants. Many of these recruits brought with them the keystones of colcha embroidery — the national popular taste for ornamentation, as well as knowledge of the stitch and designs that would later appear in the distinctive needlework of New Mexico.

Establishment and Relocation of the Capital of the Colony

Eighty carts and wagons drawn by oxen carried the provisions—tools, farming implements, food, water, bedding, armaments, clothing, boots and shoes, seeds, medicine, yard goods, and supplies for making and repairing clothing (needles, thimbles, scissors, silk thread, buttons). The cavalcade included seven thousand head of livestock — three thousand churro sheep, plus goats, pigs, cattle, oxen, horses, and mules. It also included eight Franciscan priests and two lay brothers.

In Spain, the institutions of church and state were bound together inextricably. The pope had granted Spain's Catholic monarchs dominion over the New World in exchange for their commitment to convert the native people to Christianity. Zealously honoring this commitment to what it deemed a just and honorable enterprise, the state paid the travel expenses and upkeep of the ten churchmen who went to New Mexico to establish missions and convert the Indians. Oñate footed the bill for almost everyone else.

This man of wealth and influence was an aristocrat, born in New Spain to a family whose fortune came from successful silver mines. His wife was a descendant of Hernán Cortés, who had garnered fame and the gold of the Aztecs from his exploits in what became the heart of New Spain. Oñate gambled that he could do the same. He invested his personal fortune in the hope of huge returns from the veins of gold and silver he was sure he would find and mine in the unexploited province of New Mexico.

In August 1598, after seven months of travel across hundreds of miles of desert terrain, the colonists, led by Oñate's lieutenant governor, Francisco de Sosa Peñalosa, met up with Oñate at the predetermined spot — the pueblo of Ohkay Owingeh. The Spaniards named the place San Juan in honor of Juan de Oñate's patron saint. In less than two weeks, the foundation of a temporary church was set. It was the end of summer, too late to put in crops. To survive the approaching winter, the newcomers levied food and other sustenance from the residents of the pueblo. A few months later, Oñate decided to move his settlers across the Rio Grande to the smaller pueblo of Yunque-Yunque to put some space between them and their former hosts. He named the new place San Gabriel del Yunque.

Constructed of adobe and rock, the pueblo consisted of several tiers of rooms surrounding a central plaza. The Spaniards set about occupying the southwestern corner of the four-hundred-room pueblo and remodeling it to suit their needs. Most of the Indians left and took up homes in Ohkay Owingeh. San Gabriel was now the official capital of the province of New Mexico. It had its own *cabildo* (town council) and hopes for the future.

Most colonists found the place uninviting and put minimal effort into establishing a permanent home. Some obtained grants of land and began cultivating fields upriver from San Gabriel, but most did little to improve the land. The colony never managed to grow enough to feed and sustain itself. Oñate and his fellow aristocrats had brought mining tools and equipment. They spent their time exploring for gold and silver rather than performing menial domestic tasks.

The governor and his soldier-settlers made frequent forays from San Gabriel in search of new sources of wealth. On these forays, Oñate made contact with other Indian groups and kept an eye out for an all-water route to the Pacific, which the viceroy had tasked him to find. On the plains to the east, he found large herds of buffalo. The Spaniards built a huge log corral to capture the lumbering beasts, which they hoped to domesticate and use for meat and hides, as they had the cattle of New Spain (Kessell 2002:80). Their efforts to round up and retain the uncooperative animals came to naught. The disappointed explorers abandoned their plan and moved on.

Captain Gaspar Pérez de Villagrá, an officer in the expedition who had been educated in Spain, took notes and wrote an epic poem about Oñate's enterprise. His *Historia de la Nueva México,* published in Spain in 1610, provides detailed descriptions of the exploits and tribulations of Oñate and his colony. In his *Historia,* Villagrá also documents the deeds of a remarkable woman — Doña Eufemia Peñalosa, wife of Lieutenant Governor Francisco de Sosa Peñalosa. Historian José Antonio Esquibel dubbed her the First Lady of Spanish colonial New Mexico (Esquibel 1994:28).

Doña Eufemia embodied the courage and spirit of the women who accompanied their soldier-husbands to the desolate new province. Captain Villagrá, perhaps a bit smitten, described her as "extremely beautiful" and unusual in her "splendid, quick and clear mentality." He extolled the virtue and valor of the rebuke she issued to discouraged recruits who had to use their own resources to support themselves during the long delays that beset the expedition in Santa Bárbara. Although some gave up and abandoned the effort, she managed to inspire and persuade many others to hold fast in their commitment to the expedition. The woman's bold oration that Villagrá so admired was the first of several critical contributions she made to Oñate's enterprise.

Although we have no record of her surname, Esquibel speculates that Doña Eufemia was from a wealthy and esteemed Spanish family. Her husband was born in Spain, and the couple settled in a cattle ranching community on the northern frontier of New Spain, where silver had been discovered. There, her husband acquired status and wealth, as evidenced by his rank of captain when he enlisted his family in the Oñate expedition. The inventory of equipment and provisions he planned to take was second in value to that of Oñate. His household included three African slaves, one mulatto slave, and an unspecified number of male and female servants. The couple had two sons and a daughter, and all three of them joined their parents on the expedition to New Mexico. The sons went as soldiers, and the daughter as wife of the purveyor of supplies for the expedition (Esquibel 1994:19).

Several months after the colony had relocated to San Gabriel, news came that hostile Indians were gathering to mount an attack on the Spaniards and the natives of Ohkay Owingeh Pueblo. The colony was especially vulnerable at that time because seventy soldiers had left to wage a retaliatory campaign against the Indians of Acoma Pueblo.

As Governor Oñate was busy organizing his remaining men to protect their colony, Doña Eufemia took the initiative and organized the women. Under her leadership, twenty-five wives took up arms (most likely heavy, matchlock guns called harquebuses, according to Esquibel) and positioned themselves on the rooftops of the pueblo buildings to help defend San Gabriel.

Villagrá chronicled their courageous act, although he couldn't have witnessed it because he was off participating in the Acoma campaign. He wrote that as Oñate's men rushed to their posts, someone pointed out that people were already in place on the rooftops. Oñate shouted at them, asking who they were and what they thought they were doing. Doña Eufemia replied that if he chose to order them all down, the women would comply. If not, he should leave them alone and allow them to help defend their homes. The general ordered her to continue commanding the summits. Oñate was once again indebted to the commitment and contributions of Doña Eufemia, "a dame of courage singular and spirit great" (Villagrá [1610] 1992: canto 27).

Doña Eufemia was the first Spanish woman referred to by name in the chronicles of New Mexico. After her came a long line of other adventurous women who succeeded in putting down roots and establishing homes in the remote province. We don't know them by name. Few of their deeds and accomplishments were ever recorded. But it was these brave and resilient women who set the stage upon which the needle art of colcha embroidery would later appear.

The relief expedition, which included the women, their finery, and seventy-three more soldier-colonists, arrived in San Gabriel on Christmas Eve 1600. The colonists had survived their first two winters, but living conditions were miserable. Food rationing, sickness, friction between neighbors, and harsh weather plagued the settlement.

Provisions were running out. When it became clear that there were no riches to be found, the disillusioned colonists remained only because the penalty for desertion was death. Families began requesting permission to leave. Oñate had to act decisively. He ad-

The Spanish Passion for Embroidery

Embroidered garments were an important part of life in Spain for many centuries. Spanish folk art specialist Maria Antonia Pelauzy writes that the most expressive aspect of Iberian Peninsula textiles was the rich embroidery used to decorate fabrics, bedding, the best clothes of villagers, and even the caparisons of horses and mules. She points out that the elaborately braided and embroidered suits worn by toreadors today are an enduring expression of the Spanish passion for embroidery (Pelauzy 1997:33).

Members of the Oñate expedition brought embroidered finery, as well as needles with which to make, and perhaps embellish, clothing. The manifest of Captain Don Luis de Velasco included a suit, doublet, and short cloak of chestnut-colored cloth trimmed with silver embroidery. The wealthy aristocrat also brought to the frontier weapons, horses, tack, boots, shoes, hats, handkerchiefs, mattresses and bedding, and a staggering number of suits made of Castilian satin and Chinese flowered silk (Hackett 1923: vol. 1, 429–31).

Embroidered items were also listed in inventories of the possessions of women who participated in a relief expedition dispatched in response to Oñate's plea for reinforcements for his struggling colony. Doña Francisca Galindo, a captain's wife, brought nine dresses, most made of luxury fabric (red satin, black taffeta, black satin, crimson satin, velvet, silk). The crimson satin was embroidered in gold. Even her more practical, everyday frocks had embroidered elements. A green dress of coarse cloth had sashes embroidered in gold, and a brown one had a white, embroidered skirt. Doña Francisca also brought two pillows embroidered in silk (Burke 1973:105).

opted strict and unpopular measures to discipline the colonists, going so far as to send troops under the command of soldier-poet Captain Villagrá to pursue four deserters. The troops caught up with two of them and slit their throats (Kessell 2002:80).

During the summer of 1601, Oñate headed off on an expedition with a large band of soldiers. He left Lieutenant Governor Peñalosa in charge of San Gabriel. Although Peñalosa was under strict orders to hold the colony intact, in August and September he presided over public hearings at which prominent members of the community voiced their support for abandoning the enterprise. In October 1601 he penned a letter of desperation to the viceroy, stating that they were determined to abandon the enterprise if help didn't reach the colony within five months (Esquibel 1994:26). Many settlers, including Peñalosa's sons, daughter, and son-in-law, did flee the colony around that time.

Continued misery and disappointment eventually led to mass desertion. When Oñate returned to San Gabriel, he found only twenty-five soldiers. Peñalosa was one of them, and it's likely that Doña Eufemia remained at her husband's side. Oñate imprisoned Peñalosa for not preventing the mass desertion and refused to release him until he signed a document stating that the deserters had forced him to let them go. The honorable Peñalosa refused to sign a false statement. Records fail to indicate what became of Doña Eufemia and her husband.

A final blow shattered Oñate's dream of garnering fortune and fame like the successful adventurers before him. He was suspended from office for failing to establish the colony and was recalled to New Spain. Two years before Oñate fell into disgrace, Spanish novelist and poet Miguel de Cervantes had introduced to the world the character Don Quixote — another gentleman whose quest for glory came to naught. In 1607 Oñate resigned as governor of the foundering province of New Mexico.

The king was tempted at that point to abandon the effort to colonize the distant, unprofitable province. He changed his mind only when Franciscan missionaries in New Mexico waged a successful campaign to hold onto their territory. Exaggerating their actual accomplishments at least tenfold, the churchmen appealed to the conscience of the devout monarch and begged him not to abandon the thousands of Indians they had already converted to Christianity (deBuys 1985:48). It was the Catholic faith that ensured the continuation of the colony and defined and sustained the culture out of which colcha embroidery would later emerge.

The decision to establish a royal colony in the province and maintain that colony at government expense was made for pragmatic, as well as religious, reasons. European rivals continued to encroach on Spain's stake in the New World. Englishmen of the Virginia Company had just established the colony of Jamestown, and the French were building the fur-trading post of Quebec on the Saint Lawrence River (Kessell 2002:97). The disappointing province could at least serve as a buffer to protect northern New Spain and its profitable silver mines from Spain's rivals.

In 1609 Pedro de Peralta, the first royal governor of New Mexico, chose a new site for his seat of government — a place thirty miles to the south of the old capital. Some families who had been granted land in the vicinity of the San Gabriel settlement elected to stay and farm their holdings rather than relocate. Governor Peralta escorted the rest of the settlers down to establish the new *villa* (town) of Santa Fe. The new capital of the province was located a respectful distance from the Indian pueblos — far enough removed from them to avoid conflict over land use and property.

A seat of government, the *casas reales* (royal houses), was built on one side of the town's central plaza. Nearby stood a military garrison and a chapel. The new site offered ample grazing land for sheep and other domestic animals. The stage was set for the appearance of colcha embroidery. The flocks of sheep would grow larger and provide the wool that women transformed into woven cloth and embroidery yarn. Families would learn to adapt to the arid new land and sustain themselves in small communities anchored by a Catholic church or chapel.

In fields around the new town, the settlers succeeded in planting crops from the Old World — Castilian wheat and barley, watermelons, cantaloupes, cabbages, and onions. From New Spain they added varieties of beans, chilies, and tomatoes to their fields. A stream brought water from the nearby mountains, which also provided wood for their buildings, furniture, farm implements, carts, and fuel.

The settlers who remained in the north also managed to put down roots. They spread out from San Gabriel into today's Española Valley, built simple houses, and grew food for their families in the alluvial plain beside the river. By 1680 the sprawling jurisdiction of New Mexico consisted of the capital of Santa Fe, plus small agricultural settlements and communities scattered along the Rio Grande from Socorro to Taos (Sagel 1983:7).

Homes were simple in construction and sixteenth-century Spanish in design. Walls were built of stone or adobes, large bricks made of mud mixed with sand and straw as a binder. To make the adobes, settlers shoveled the mud mixture into rectangular frames, dried the bricks until they held their shape, unmolded them, turned them on edge, and allowed them to dry for several days. Settlers also felled large pine trees and dragged the logs down from the mountains. The logs were laid wall to wall as support for a roof of closely placed branches covered by layers of smaller branches, brush, and mud.

The width of a room was limited to the length of available log beams. Historian E. Boyd has speculated that the typical house had two or three rooms, one of which was a relatively large multipurpose room (Boyd 1974:7). Women cooked the family's meals in the kitchen fireplace, as well as in outdoor pits and beehive-shaped adobe *hornos* (ovens) — a heritage from the Muslim occupation of southern Spain.

The kitchen fireplace was in a corner or against a wall, as in Spain. Post beams that may have supported a fireplace hood above a cooking hearth were found during excavations at the Palace of the Governors in Santa Fe (Post 2006:90). Adjacent postholes may have housed beams that

Taos, NM, The Penitente Morada. *Photo by John C. Collier, Jr., 1943. Courtesy New Mexico Museum of Art. New Mexico Farm Security Administration, museum purchase with funds from the Pinewood Foundation, with additional support from Barbara Erdman, 1990 (1990.70.206).*

A woman in Chimayó, New Mexico, baking bread in a horno, early 1900s. Courtesy Menaul Historical Library, Prudence Clark Collection (1975.001.043).

held up an elevated shelf or "shepherd's bed," where someone could have slept near the fire. Others in the household probably slept on the floor on sheep pelts, buffalo hides, or sacks filled with wool.

Fireplaces provided warmth and light. Candles were scarce and were generally reserved for religious observances. Wood was the most important resource. From it the colonists fashioned furnishings for their homes, as well as carts and farm implements. Iron was scarce, so iron implements were treasured items. Scissors and the iron *comal* for cooking tortillas were bequeathed in wills and handed down through the generations.

Clothing in the frontier province included embroidered items. When he appeared before Inquisitors at a hearing in 1663, thirty-six-year-old Nicolas de Aguilar — a resident of New Mexico who had lived there for twenty-six years — was wearing buckskin shoes and a doublet of white cloth embroidered with blue wool. A list of personal effects he brought with him to the hearing included a badly worn woolen doublet with sleeves embroidered with blue wool, and a cotton shirt embroidered with dark red wool. Among his other effects were an antelope skin muffler, a cloth containing roots for curing fevers and healing wounds, two wool sheets, several books, and a rosary with a small silver cross (Hackett 1923: vol. 3, 139 – 40).

Spain Loses and Recovers the Province

Because of its formidable distance from the heart of New Spain, the supply-starved colony waged a continuous battle for existence. A caravan of heavy-duty freight wagons laden with staples and gear for the missions, mail, assorted officials, and an occasional colonist arrived from Mexico City every third year. Historian Marc Simmons points out that the deliveries were five and six years apart during the early years of operation (Simmons 2001:3). The trip to New Mexico took six months, and the usual round-trip lasted a year and a half.

Few new colonists arrived during the middle of the seventeenth century. Kessell estimates that the population of the province of New Mexico at its peak in the 1660s, excluding the native Indians, was no more than twenty-five hundred. By contrast, the population of the prosperous mining town of Zacatecas in northern New Spain in 1667 was nearly sixteen thousand (Kessell 2002:110). Santa Fe was the only official town in New Mexico.

Most of its soldiers, residents, and even some government officials were illiterate and unable to sign their names.

One notable exception was Doña Teresa de Aguilera y Roche, the well-bred daughter of a Spanish diplomat. Born and raised in Italy, she married Bernardo López de Mendizábal, who was appointed governor of New Mexico in 1658. Arriving in Santa Fe with a carriage, bed, writing desk, fancy clothes, linens, and a small collection of books, this educated woman came to be viewed with suspicion and hostility. Servants observed her reading books with strange writing and laughing as she read them. They concluded that the books must be heretical in nature. Based on this and other serious charges, a commissary of the Inquisition arrested the couple in 1662. They were taken to be tried in Mexico City—victims of ignorance, superstition, and the ongoing struggle between the church and the state for Indian labor during the seventeenth century in New Mexico.

Mendizábal himself was no paragon of virtue. Like other governors before him, he came to New Mexico for personal gain. Before leaving New Spain, he purchased large quantities of textiles, sugar, shoes, and other staples that he could market profitably in the supply-starved community. He shipped the goods to Santa Fe and set up a store in the casas reales. There he traded his imported wares for local goods, which he then sent with emissaries to be traded in the mining communities of northern New Spain. His commercial enterprise in the casas reales included an illegal sweatshop that used Indian labor to weave textiles (Scholes 1937:380).

We know from records of disputes over payment that the governor employed women colonists to weave cloth, make stockings, and do drawn work and embroidery on shirts and piece goods (Scholes 1937:390). He may well have instructed his workers to replicate the patterns and style of embroidered items in the wardrobe of his sophisticated wife, Doña Teresa. The greedy governor's confidence that there was a market for embroidered goods testifies to the status and enduring presence of embroidery during the seventeenth century in New Mexico.

The practice of embroidery — and just about everything else in the province that was Spanish — suffered a cataclysmic disruption toward the end of the century. Boiling over with resentment at decades of repression of their families, their culture, and their native religion, the Indians living along the upper Rio Grande joined forces and drove out the col-

Churro Sheep

Spanish churro sheep helped sustain the colonial enterprise in New Mexico during the seventeenth century and continued to play an important role in the economy and everyday life of the province for several centuries. The fleece of the churro would be transformed into the ground fabric and yarn that Spanish colonial women in the province used for their colcha embroidery.

Churros, an ancient and hardy Iberian breed, were brought from the south of Spain to New Spain in the early 1500s. There was a rapid buildup of the sheep and weaving industries in New Spain within thirty years after the founding of Mexico City.

Coronado brought churros on his expedition to New Mexico in 1540. Oñate's cavalcade of colonists and provisions in 1598 also included churros. The stalwart little sheep adapted well to the high desert. They could go without water for several days and survive by grazing the sparse vegetation of the arid province. When he was suspended from office in 1607, Oñate turned over to Governor Peralta a thousand sheep and goats, probably a total for the entire colony (Minge 1979:10).

The convoy of colonists that fled to El Paso in the wake of the Pueblo Revolt managed to take along a number of sheep, goats, and cows (Kessell 2002:121). One historian speculates that had the refugees not succeeded in herding their churros to El Paso, the colony there may have perished for lack of food (Minge 1979:10).

In the course of recapturing New Mexico in 1694, Governor Vargas attacked a rebellious group of Indians above the canyons of Cochiti, south of Santa Fe. He captured prisoners, horses, and—to his great surprise—more than nine hundred churros (Minge 1979:10). The Spanish had taught the Indians quite a lot about animal husbandry during the years before the Pueblo Revolt, and the Indians were careful to preserve the animals they had come to value when they burned and eradicated every other vestige of Spanish culture.

onists and churchmen in 1680. A loosely knit coalition of several thousand Pueblo warriors attacked, burned, and destroyed the mission churches and outlying farming settlements. In six weeks of rampage, the warriors massacred 15 percent of the colony—more than 380 Spanish settlers and twenty-one out of thirty-two Franciscan missionaries. Terrified survivors from the sprawling, defenseless settlements fled to Santa Fe for protection. But the Indians had besieged the capital. The governor managed to break through the siege and lead his band of 1,946 desperate refugees three hundred miles down the Rio Grande to safety in El Paso.

A churro ready for shearing. Photo by Nancy C. Benson.

Nowhere else in the New World had native people managed to take back an entire province. The Pueblo Revolt of 1680 was a humiliating defeat for Spain. Out of pride, as well as the need to protect the empire's richer settlements in northern New Spain, the king issued orders to take back the province. To accomplish this feat, the viceroy of New Spain chose Don Diego de Vargas, a member of one of Spain's leading families who had fought for his country in Europe before moving to the New World.

The newly appointed governor and captain general of New Mexico marched north from El Paso in 1692 with two hundred soldiers and two cannons. He managed to regain the allegiance of twenty-three pueblos without firing a shot and returned to El Paso. In the fall of 1693 he led the first wave of colonists and priests back to reclaim the capital of Santa Fe.

Seventy families made the return trip up the Rio Grande. Weakened by lean years as refugees, thirty women and children died on the punishing journey. When the diminished group finally reached Santa Fe, they found that the Indians had changed their minds. They renounced the allegiance they had given Vargas the year before and refused to withdraw from the casas reales. The Spanish set up camp outside of town, tried to negotiate, and by the end of December 1693 had managed to retake their capital by force.

During their thirteen-year occupation of the buildings, the Indians had remade the Spanish seat of government into a pueblo. They had remodeled it to suit their needs, as Oñate had done to the Indian pueblo of Yunque-Yunque when creating his capital of San

Gabriel. According to Vargas scholar John Kessell, the Indians piled third and fourth stories onto the Spanish structure. They subdivided the large interior rooms into more compact, Pueblo-style living and storage spaces (Kessell 2004:29).

Once again the Spanish seat of government, the complex in Santa Fe was already teeming with people when the next wave of colonists—mostly farmers and artisans—arrived in June 1694. An incident from the court records of that year adds a bit of continuity to the biography of colcha embroidery. Some clever individual executed a clandestine heist of what must have been a valued commodity — yarn — although the balance of the haul consisted of soap and chilies. Through an unlocked trapdoor, the thief had sneaked from upstairs rooms into one of Vargas's storage units on a plaza inside the complex (Kessell 2004:29). Was it a skein of plain, undyed yarn that the thief risked punishment for stealing? Or was it perhaps an appealing skein of yarn, dyed an attractive indigo blue or a bright yellow, that someone wanted to use to embroider a special design on a garment?

The New Town of Santa Cruz

Vargas wasted no time in expanding the Spanish presence in the province. After securing Santa Fe, he focused on repopulating the area of the San Gabriel settlement — one of the locales where colcha embroidery would subsequently flourish. He sent a reconnaissance party back up to the area of the original settlement. The leader reported that on the bank of the river they found a house and buildings that had once belonged to a Miguel Lujan. The buildings were still intact, and there was a family living in them.

Two groups — the San Lazaro and San Cristobal Indians — had moved into the area after the Pueblo Revolt. Vargas forced the Indians to vacate the villages and land they had appropriated and removed them to other pueblos. In April 1695, having secured the area for resettlement, he proclaimed Santa Cruz de la Cañada to be the second official villa in the province of New Mexico and notified forty-four families in Santa Fe that they were to proceed to Santa Cruz and establish the town. The new villa was located on the south side of the Santa Cruz River at the site of the vacated pueblo of San Lazaro. Vargas led the settlers north, granted them formal possession of their lands, and sent nineteen more families to join them the following year.

When the settlers arrived, they found they had been granted houses and cleared fields — complete with dams and irrigation ditches — that the Indians had been using. But even with such unprecedented advantages, the settlers at first had difficulty sustaining themselves. Their tools were inadequate, the soil was difficult to work, and their crops failed. Residents complained to the governor that poisonous weeds were killing their livestock. And the place still wasn't safe. Indians had killed five missionaries and twenty-one colonists, and a small-scale revolt had broken out just north of their new villa.

Spanish law imposed severe restrictions on the movements of all citizens. A special permit was required to travel from one settlement to another. In 1696 residents of Santa Cruz petitioned their governor to allow them to relocate to a new site with better land and more security. Their petition came to naught. The penalty for desertion was so great that most families decided to stay put and try to make the best of their situation.

In the years immediately after Vargas's successful reconquest of the frontier province, the Spanish government continued to allow groups of settlers to move to New Mexico. Thereafter, the arrival of settlers from the population centers of New Spain slowed to a trickle. New Mexicans found themselves left largely alone. Although they continued to be influenced by the larger Spanish culture of which they were a part, they began to develop their own style of life in the far-flung province.

By the end of the seventeenth century, the stage was set for the emergence of an embroidery that was uniquely New Mexican. Images of the needlework on dresses, doublets, shirts, and other personal items brought by the earliest settlers lived on in the minds and hearts of those who came after them. Flocks of hardy little churro sheep from the arid lands of Spain had adapted well and grown larger in the high desert of the far northern frontier. And strong, independent women, who took considerable pride in their Hispanic values, faith, and traditions, had transported their culture to a harsh, distant land and put down roots.

CHAPTER 2
1700s: Early Colcha Embroideries

Families in the settlements along the upper Rio Grande were left pretty much to themselves during the eighteenth century. Children of those families married neighbors and produced children of their own. The population of the province grew, and as it grew it became increasingly native in character. This change took several generations, but late in the second half of the century there emerged a distinct new culture — Hispanic New Mexican. The earliest colcha embroideries were a product of that new culture.

During the first half of the century, as the new culture was coming into focus, New Mexicans continued to relish colorful, embroidered finery. They had brought needles to make, mend, and decorate their clothing. Most of the luggage of colonists in the 1693 Vargas expedition to New Mexico consisted of clothing, blankets, fabrics, trimmings, and thread, including silk embroidery floss.

When Vargas died in 1704, the inventory of his possessions included seven pounds of silk for sewing, as well as six pounds of floss silk and seven and a half pounds of silk for buttonholes. His estate also included two locally made elk-skin sword belts embroidered with silk; a raisin-colored suit embroidered "in the old-fashioned style," with two pairs of embroidered breeches; and two embroidered standards (Kessell et al. 2002:236 – 42).

Opposite: A silk shawl embroidered with silk thread, late eighteenth or early nineteenth century. Shawls from Asia arrived in Spain and New Spain via the Manila galleons. Courtesy Museum of Spanish Colonial Art, Collections of the Spanish Colonial Arts Society, Inc., Santa Fe. Gift of Catherine F. Bieber (1963.15).

The three items of highest value in the estate of a trader who died in 1726 were a coverlet from Toluca, a cloak from Seville, and a waistcoat for a woman. Other high-value items included a fine silk shawl, a length of red taffeta, a short cloak of red satin, another coverlet, a blanket for a bed, and a mattress (Ahlborn 1983:43).

It's tempting to speculate that the high-value coverlets, silk shawl, and woman's waistcoat that the trader left to his heirs were embellished with decorative, detailed embroidery. Most New Mexicans were familiar with embroideries produced in New Spain for both domestic and religious use. And in both Spain and New Spain, the passion for embroidered finery certainly hadn't cooled at this point.

In addition to being inspired by legacy items and trade goods that bore the images of their own culture, Hispanic women in eighteenth-century New Mexico may have been inspired to compete with the finery of their Pueblo neighbors. Spanish administrators in 1744 appraised the estate of one Maria Calabacita, a baptized, unmarried woman of Santo Domingo Pueblo, south of Santa Fe. Her estate included an embroidered shawl, a painted shawl, a damask shawl with blue and scarlet ribbons, and a red silk cap decorated with a plume and gold raised-work embroidery.

A red cloth shawl decorated with lace and wide ribbons of red and yellow was the item of greatest value — forty-five pesos — in her entire estate. A coral bracelet with twenty strands and two amulets of jet was worth twenty-five pesos (Ahlborn 1983:44). In stark contrast with the luxury items, her mare and cow were valued at fifteen pesos each. Her sheep and lambs were worth only two pesos apiece. It's also interesting to note that a record of court proceedings just a few years before her death indicated that one week's wages for a day laborer was six pesos, the value of just one of the Indian woman's embroidered, well-worn shawls.

In 1745 the governor of New Mexico spent four months visiting communities to hear grievances. Most of the complaints had to do with the exchange of locally made goods (Minge 1979:18). The goods ranged from embroidered shoes and embroidered cotton *mantas* (blankets) to boots and woolen stockings. A resident of Isleta Pueblo asked the governor to help him collect from a man the eight sheep and two cows he was to receive in exchange for a colcha. When we apply to the Isleta man's claim the values assessed the previous year for the estate of Maria Calabacita (two pesos per sheep and fifteen pesos per

Embroidered Bedcovers: A Spanish Custom

An essay on popular furniture by Carlos Pinel in the San Antonio Museum of Art's exhibition catalog *Folk Art of Spain and the Americas, El Alma del Pueblo* sheds light on the Spanish practice of decorating the family's bedding. Pinel explains that the custom of the dressed bed came into fashion during the Middle Ages in Spain, when furniture and walls in the homes of the wealthy were covered with fabrics or tapestries to keep the sleeper warm and keep out drafts (Pinel 1997:88).

The dressed bed, complete with handmade bedcover, stood on a dais and sometimes had a frame with supports covered by curtains. Fine embroidery or lace was often hung over the front. Pinel found that the richest popular embroidery was done in multicolored silk and wool with floral and animal designs.

Spanish folk craft scholar Maria Antonia Pelauzy notes that a profusion of needlework had always adorned shirts, sheets, decorative pillows, altar cloths, coverlets, and towels in Spanish homes (Pelauzy 1978:31). Much of the plain fabric woven in the home was used to make coverlets, which usually received an embroidered design—generally a floral theme. The edges of the coverlets were trimmed with fringe or crocheted strips (Pelauzy 1978:16). An eighteenth-century bed covering from Salamanca, Spain, in the Museo Nacional de Antropologia in Madrid is made of wool that has been elaborately embroidered with the tree of life—a motif commonly associated with marriage.

cow), it becomes clear that his colcha was a highly desirable item. It was worth the equivalent of forty-six pesos.

In 1764 a man filed a legal suit in Santa Fe. He asked restitution for a rare colcha that another man had borrowed from his wife six years before. The plaintiff claimed that the colcha, described as embroidered Chinese silk, had received bad treatment and needed cleaning. In 1765 the estate of a merchant who died in Albuquerque included an old colcha, a large number of woven articles, and an ample stock of sewing needles (Minge 1979:19).

A Distinctive New Mexican Embroidery

Records that testify to the existence of a distinctive local embroidery appeared in New Mexico during the second half of the eighteenth century. Creating something both useful and beautiful would certainly have added joy to the lives of weary, hardworking women in the harsh and desolate province. By embroidering a solid layer of designs in yarn on her wool coverlet, for example, a woman added warmth and visual appeal to something she would use and enjoy every day.

This embroidery was done with hand-spun wool on a ground of loosely woven wool called *sabanilla*. The stitching covered the sabanilla completely with floral or geometric designs. One stitch — a couching technique that came to be called the colcha stitch — was used to the exclusion of all others. Although few if any examples of local embroidery done in the eighteenth century have survived the ravages of time, it is thought that the colcha stitch has been used in New Mexico since the mid-1700s (Gavin 1994:70).

One of the earliest records of the embroidery is in the list of furnishings of Spanish churches, chapels, and Indian missions that Fray Francisco Dominguez compiled during his visit to New Mexico in 1776. He noted four embroidered coverlets in the inventory of the sacristy of the military chapel at Santa Fe. And on the steps of the sanctuary of the church in Santa Cruz, he found one colcha with white flowers on a dark background (Boyd 1974:213).

The Santa Cruz church was completed in 1748, and the bishop from New Spain who administered churches in New Mexico visited it in 1760. He noted that the building was large but lacked adornment (Sagel 1983:13). Fray Andrés García, a friar who served at

Opposite: Altar cloth by Beatrice Maestas Sandoval, 41 by 84 inches. The piece won Best of Show at Spanish Market in Santa Fe in 2000. The Spanish custom of embroidering on items for religious use continues to this day in New Mexico. Photo by Dan Richey.

Evolution of the Term Colcha in New Mexico

It's not unusual for words to shift in meaning over time and when used in different locations. Such is the case for the term *colcha,* according to Josie Caruso, an independent scholar and textile restorer. Caruso points out that the word, which in Spain referred to a quilt (and by extension to a bedspread), has broadened in meaning over three centuries to become a term strongly associated with a style of embroidery in northern New Mexico.

Although it's difficult to trace this shift with precision, documentary evidence does provide clues. The 1704 inventory of the possessions of Diego de Vargas included *una colcha azul de algodon de china* (one blue cotton bedspread from China) and *una colcha de lama de china encarnada forrada en mitan verde* (one bedspread of red Chinese lamé, lined with green pressed linen). Spanish bedspreads were often embroidered, but the term *bordada* ("embroidered"), which describes other items in the Vargas inventory, is not applied to these two bedspreads. Estate inventories of other New Mexicans in the early eighteenth century do include embroidered bedspreads, which were generally of high value.

By 1742 the term *colcha* appears outside the context of bedding. A friar at the Santa Ana Pueblo mission church in New Mexico writes that he has "placed a curtain before the picture of Lady St. Anne, which is a colcha from Tlascalteca" (Boyd 1974:210). This colcha may or may not have been embroidered.

Later in the 1700s, however, the association of colcha with embroidery is evident in artwork and documents. Paintings done in New Spain during this century depict embroidered carpets in domestic settings and, more often, associated with altars and religious figures. Many of the carpets are far too large to have been originally made as bedspreads. The Santa Cruz church inventory of 1779 includes an embroidered carpet on the steps of the sanctuary. Colchas are again mentioned in the 1787 inventory, both as a carpet for the high altar and in the chapel of Saint Francis. The 1828 inventory of the San Miguel del Vado chapel includes a colcha used as a carpet on feast days.

Between 1838 and 1848, colchas appear on lists of goods exported from New Mexico to Mexico. Some of these colchas may have been bedspreads made from cotton yardage and embroidered with plied commercial yarn. The commercial yarn and yardage were imported to New Mexico from the United States over the newly opened Santa Fe Trail.

A revival of Spanish colonial arts and crafts in the 1930s, promoted primarily by English-speaking patrons, resulted in further evolution of the term. New terms combining English and Spanish came into use. *Colcha knot* described the couching stitch used in traditional embroidery. *Colcha embroidery* became the term for any textile decorated with that stitch. The consensus in literature of the period was that *colcha* traditionally meant "embroidered bedspread."

The original meaning of the term *colcha*—"bedspread"—is still used in northern New Mexico. But a second meaning—one associated with embroidery—has given rise to an array of local expressions: "colcha artists" use the "colcha stitch" to embroider "colcha designs" on "colchas" of all shapes and sizes. And those "colchas" are rarely bedspreads.

Santa Cruz between 1765 and 1768, set to work and remedied that situation. A gifted woodcarver and painter, Fray García used his talents to create religious images and an elaborate altar screen to beautify the new building.

A widow named Antonia Serna had donated the land on which the church was built. We can speculate that other devout women of the parish, perhaps inspired by Fray García's spate of artistic activity, were eager to make their own contributions. By 1782 church records list another colcha — one of dark multicolored wool. The inventory of 1787 included two more new colchas, one for the chapel of Saint Francis and "a new colcha which serves as the carpet for the high altar which was given by a pious woman" (Boyd 1974:213).

A colcha in the collection of the Museum of Spanish Colonial Art in Santa Fe may have been made during the eighteenth century in Santa Cruz. This textile is covered with coarse embroidery on loosely woven (thirteen threads per inch) sabanilla. The colcha features a heraldic double-headed eagle with the heart-shaped emblem of the confraternity of Our Lady of Carmel, a religious lay organization established in Santa Cruz in 1760. A friar drew the same emblem on the title page of the account books of the confraternity. Boyd surmises that a woman saw the emblem and incorporated the image in her needlework design. As an act of devotion, she then offered the colcha to adorn the chapel of Our Lady of Carmel in the church (Boyd 1974:213).

Although the earliest records of colcha embroidery suggest a point of origin in Santa Cruz, a report written by a Franciscan friar in 1778 indicates that the practice of embroidery in the province was probably more widespread. Father Juan Agustín de Morfí was born in Spain and ordained in Mexico City. The well-traveled churchman had earned a reputation as an authority on frontier matters and served as a consultant to the royal government (Simmons 1991:128).

He wrote a report entitled "Account of Disorders in New Mexico, 1778," which described the difficulties faced by settlers in the poor and remote province. The report also provided an enthusiastic testimonial to the quality of local embroidery. The friar saw colchas that in their variety of design and beauty of color and embroidery were much better than those of Puebla and San Miguel El Grande, which were widely used in New Spain. He also saw a pillowcase made of very finely spun thread and with very delicate needlework (Simmons 1991:139). In addition to admiring the beauty of the New Mexican colchas, Father Morfí pointed out that embroidered clothing was one of the standard products that New Mexicans offered in exchange for trade goods from Spain and New Spain (Simmons 1991:133).

The same year Father Morfí submitted his report, the Continental Congress of the United States of America adopted its Articles of Confederation. Settlers in colonies on the eastern seaboard of North America had declared their independence from England and established their own government. General George Washington was struggling at Valley Forge to shape the army of the Continental Congress into a cohesive fighting force to wage a war for independence. In the next century, the new nation would expand westward and dramatically alter the lifestyle and practices of most New Mexicans.

Opposite: This solidly embroidered colcha (undyed and vegetal-dyed yarn on sabanilla) may have been made in Santa Cruz in the late eighteenth century. Courtesy Museum of Spanish Colonial Art, Collections of the Spanish Colonial Arts Society, Inc., Santa Fe (1957.41).

Spinning and Weaving in New Mexico

Women in New Mexico did much of their embroidery on sabanilla, cloth made from the fleece of churro sheep. From the original churros brought by the Oñate expedition, the flocks had grown in size. By the end of the eighteenth century, wool was abundant in the province. In 1803 alone, New Mexicans exported some twenty-six thousand sheep to Nueva Vizcaya and various Spanish frontier presidios.

The looms in New Mexico were locally produced versions of the European treadle loom. Joe Ben Wheat, an authority on southwestern weaving, wrote that the use of the treadle loom was confirmed by a 1638 invoice for a cargo of cloth produced in the Santa Fe workshop of Governor Luis de Rosas. The cargo included nineteen pieces of a coarse woolen cloth; each piece was one hundred *varas* long (a vara is approximately thirty-three inches). A piece of this length would have been impossible to make on the Pueblo vertical loom (Wheat 2003:111).

Cordova, Rio Arriba County, NM. *Photo by John C. Collier, Jr., 1943. Flocks of sheep were a mainstay of the rural New Mexico economy until well into the twentieth century. Courtesy New Mexico Museum of Art. New Mexico Farm Security Administration, museum purchase with funds from the Pinewood Foundation, with additional support from Barbara Erdman, 1990 (1990.70.321).*

Records that document the abuses of Governor Luis de Rosas testify to the existence of *telarillos,* small horizontal treadle looms. This greedy gentleman maintained a commercial weaving operation for his own profit, as would Governor López de Mendizábal less than two decades later. In the governor's sweatshop, Indian workers were forced to labor in virtual servitude. Numerous complaints against Rosas, including that he confiscated looms owned by private citizens, were lodged in 1641. The governor of the province had effectively monopolized local textile production by seizing the looms of local residents to supplement the output from the larger treadle looms in his workshop.

Women in Chimayó, New Mexico, use hand spindles to spin raw fleece into yarn in the early 1900s. Courtesy Menaul Historical Library, Prudence Clark Collection (1975.001.050).

New Mexicans spun the wool for weaving on one of two devices: the *torno ahilado* (upright spinning wheel) or a hand spindle variously referred to as a *huso* or *malacate*. The hand spindle is a slender stick with a small disk a few inches from the bottom. It is twirled upright, with its lower point resting in a bowl. More affluent households, such as that of Miguel Lucero, *alcalde mayor* of Albuquerque, used the spinning wheel. His will, executed in 1766, includes two spinning wheels and one loom with two new pairs of wool cards (Spanish Archives of New Mexico, Series 1, 3:327).

A couple in Chimayó, New Mexico, uses a home treadle loom, early 1900s. Courtesy Menaul Historical Library, Prudence Clark Collection (1975.001.051).

The long-stapled wool of the churro was ideal for home spinning and weaving. Women made the plain-weave sabanilla into sheets, mattress sacks, and bedcovers. The fabric they produced ranged from twenty-two to twenty-eight inches in width, and they joined three widths of it together to make a bedcover.

By 1760 there is evidence of the gradual acceptance of local New Mexican weaving, even by those who were wealthy enough to afford the expensive fabrics that traders imported from New Spain. The estate of a well-to-do Albuquerque woman in 1762 included a number of items woven locally: a colcha, the sack for a *colchón* (mattress), and two wool sheets. The woman's other possessions included a silver tray from Guadalajara , silver dishes from Puebla, copper and iron utensils, several hundred sheep, and ninety bundles of wool (Minge 1979:19).

The 1729 estate inventory of Diego Marquéz, an affluent resident of Santa Cruz who lived in a seven-room house, included a bed with one mattress, a Chinese linen sheet, a wool sheet, a colcha, and two pillows (Spanish Archives of New Mexico, Series 1, 3:742). A less-affluent resident of Santa Cruz, Lugarda Quintana, who died in 1749, left her heirs much simpler bedding — a mattress and two sheets (Spanish Archives of New Mexico, Series 1, 5:717). Petrona de Cárdenas, who died in Santa Cruz in 1767, left no bedding. She had fourteen children and few worldly possessions (Spanish Archives of New Mexico, Series 1, 1:1393). Her family may well have slept on the floor on *zaleas* (sheepskins). She left her heirs one cross and eight *santos* (images of saints) — a testimony to the faith that had helped the poor woman endure what must have been a hard life in northern New Mexico.

The New Mexico Colcha Stitch

Women of the culture that emerged during the second half of the eighteenth century in New Mexico used a distinctive stitching technique. That technique was based on one, and only one, stitch: the colcha stitch. The colcha is a self-couching stitch, in which a long stitch is fastened down by one or more tiny anchor stitches that secure the long stitch to the sabanilla at regular intervals. The next long stitch is placed parallel to the previous one and close enough that little or no sabanilla shows through between the adjacent stitches. The stitching flows in various directions and eventually covers the entire surface of the sabanilla.

Kay Staniland, former curator of clothing and textiles at the Museum of London, notes that the couching stitch appears on a fragment of wool dating to the first century BC. The fragment was excavated in northern Mongolia but is believed to have originated in Iran (Staniland 1991:40). She believes that the couching technique was already of considerable age in the eleventh century. She supports that claim by pointing to a large textile made in the bor-

Cloth from Eighteenth-Century New Mexico

Moths, wear and tear, and changes in style over the centuries took their toll on most wool textiles. Few from eighteenth-century New Mexico have survived, although a curious series of events brought to light two examples. E. Boyd recounts the pious acts that led to their discovery.

It seems that in 1759 the governor of New Mexico decided to have two Franciscan missionaries exhumed from Pueblo mission churches, where they had been buried the previous century. He had the bones of the friars wrapped in new habits and placed in a stone sarcophagus that was inserted at eye level in the wall of the parish church in Santa Fe. The governor intended to have these exemplary men serve as a reminder that encouraged citizens of the capital to be more devout.

The sarcophagus was opened in 1957, when it was moved to a new location in the then-enlarged Saint Francis Cathedral. Officials found that the bones of the friars had been wrapped in two different textiles in 1759. Both are dyed a deep indigo blue. One is a finely woven diagonal twill. The other is a plain-weave wool homespun. The plain-weave homespun has twelve warps and fourteen wefts per centimeter (Boyd 1974:181).

The Colcha Stitch

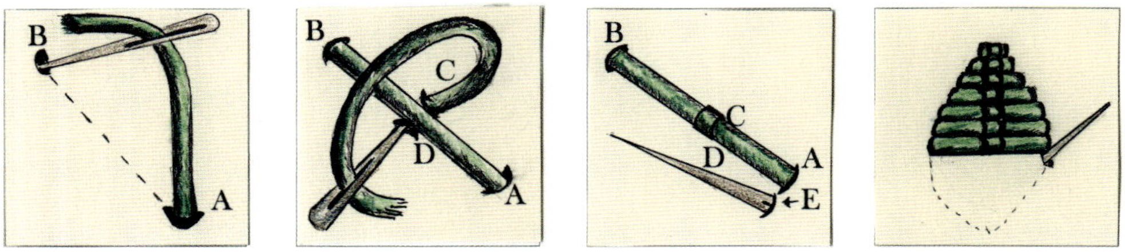

1. Up at A, down at B.
2. Up at C, down at D.
3. Up at E, then repeat steps 1 and 2.
4. The colcha stitch used in a leaf motif.

The colcha stitch—step by step. Illustration by Doris Parry.

der country of Spain in the eleventh century — variously called the Genesis or Creation hanging. The twelve-by-fifteen-foot textile has a red wool ground entirely covered with couched, colored wool and white linen thread to form a bold design. The hanging is the property of the Gerona Cathedral in Spain (Harris 1993:200).

Masterpieces that survive in cathedral treasuries give the mistaken impression that early medieval embroideries were luxury items restricted to the wealthy. Staniland believes that simpler forms of embroidery were widely used in secular, as well as religious, work. And we still have a dramatic example of the couching stitch in a secular work: the Bayeux Tapestry. This famous medieval embroidery, which provides an account of the Norman conquest of England in 1066, uses couched wool threads to give solid form to the figures in the narrative — the men, their horses, and their ships — so that they stand out from the linen ground. Staniland believes that the Bayeux Tapestry represents a large body of secular work that is now lost, and bears witness to a high level of competence and interpretative skill in the use of the couching technique (Staniland 1991:40).

There were thriving professional embroidery workshops in the capitals of Europe well before Spain established colonies in the New World. The Spanish brought wool, silk, and looms to New Spain, and in 1534 Sancho García de Larraval, a master embroiderer and nephew of a bishop, arrived to teach embroidery to the Indians. In 1546 the first embroidery guild was established in Mexico City. The guilds included both Spanish and Indian craftsmen, who produced elaborate vestments, altar cloths, and other church textiles, as well as fabrics and clothing for secular use. Men in monasteries and women in convents also produced rich embroideries (Pierce 1996:144). In the collection of the Victoria and Albert Museum in London is an elaborately embroidered outer garment that belonged to a church official. The garment, made in Spain during the late sixteenth or early seventeenth century and acquired in Mexico, includes the couching stitch.

Embroidery was considered an important part of a young woman's education in New Spain. Nuns were dispatched from Spain as early as 1530 to help with the education of Indian girls, and by 1534 there were eight girls' schools in New Spain. These schools emphasized moral education and taught household tasks, including sewing and embroidering (Ricard 1966:210).

There is ample evidence in paintings that the practice of embroidery, including the couching stitch, was widespread in New Spain in the eighteenth century. A painting done there in 1773 depicts a textile on the floor that appears to be solidly embroidered with couching stitches. The textile is finished with a fringe that is characteristically Spanish (Pelauzy 1978:35). This fringe comprises blocks of color used in the embroidery.

A painting in the book *Pintura y Vida Cotidiana en Mexico, 1650 – 1950* depicts a religious subject in a domestic setting and shows the same type of textile. The textile appears to be solidly embroidered with couch-

Our Lady of Guadalupe, 1773, *by Andreas de Islas. Paintings done in New Spain during the eighteenth century show that embroidered, fringed floor coverings were used in both religious and domestic settings. Courtesy Figge Art Museum, Davenport, Iowa. Gift of C. A. Ficke (25.159).*

An altar cloth embroidered in a convent in New Spain during the late eighteenth century. The work features silk and metallic embroidery thread on hand-spun linen. Courtesy Museum of Spanish Colonial Art, Collections of the Spanish Colonial Arts Society, Inc., Santa Fe (1965.25).

ing stitches; its fringe comprises blocks of color used in the embroidery. The painting also shows a version of the Spanish dressed bed, complete with a canopy and drapery.

A painting in the book *Casta Painting: Images of Race in Eighteenth-Century Mexico,* by Ilona Katzew, shows yet another embroidered floor covering that has a fringe of the same colors used in the embroidery. What little fringe remains on a New Mexico colcha made between 1790 and 1850 also exhibits blocks of colors that are the same as those used in the embroidery.

The most likely theory is that the New Mexico colcha stitch — like the majority of New Mexico settlers — came directly from New Spain. The Witte Museum in San Antonio has a bedspread made in Mexico; several designs on the elaborately embroidered bedspread are done in the couching stitch. Another theory, congruent with the first, is that the New Mexico colcha stitch may have come from China. Chinese silk embroidery with delicate little couching stitches in combination with other stitches was a highly desirable trade item that found its way to New Mexico via the Manila galleons (Boyd 1974:210).

Spain had colonized the Philippines in the 1500s. It established a sea trade route that connected the islands with the motherland by way of New Spain. The Spanish government

Wool-on-wool colcha, 1790–1850. Photo by Blair Clark. Courtesy International Folk Art Foundation Collection at the Museum of International Folk Art (DCA), Santa Fe (FA.67.43.4).

negotiated agreements with Chinese traders to deliver large quantities of silks to the port of Manila. From 1565 until 1815, galleons laden with embroidered shawls, Chinese porcelain, spices, and painted cotton fabric (chintz) from India sailed to the west coast port of Acapulco. The cargo then traveled by mule train to Mexico City, heart of the viceroyalty of New Spain and principal market for the cargo. (The 1597 manifest of Captain Don Luis de Velasco, a participant in the Oñate expedition, shows that he brought a suit of Chinese flowered silk to New Mexico.) The balance of the cargo continued overland to the east coast port of Veracruz, then by ship to markets in Spain.

Of the cargo acquired by traders in Mexico City, a small fraction was eventually carted up to markets on the northern frontier and from there found its way to New Mexico. When the Santa Fe Convention Center was razed in 2007, archaeologists examining the excavated site identified the ruins of a hacienda that appeared on a map made in 1767. Around the hacienda of what must have been an upscale rural family, they found pottery that had been imported via New Spain — some from as far away as the Philippines (Garcia 2007:8).

Independent trade caravans from Mexico City plied their way north on the Camino Real, passing through markets in Chihuahua and El Paso on their way to Santa Fe. The trade caravans brought imported Chinese and Philippine embroideries, as well as painted chintz from India. Donna Pierce points out that the curvilinear floral motifs on this popular fabric appear on early fabrics and embroideries made in Spain and New Spain. Indeed, textile patterns all over the Western world echoed those popular designs in the late eighteenth century (Pierce and Weigle 1996:144). The painted chintz was surely a source of ideas and inspiration for New Mexico women who did colcha embroidery.

The Distinct New Culture Endures

Travel to New Mexico was slow because roads were poor, the distance between major population centers was great, and a permit was required for travel within the kingdom. But New Mexicans were never as acutely isolated as portrayed in some history books. A convoy of several hundred New Mexicans armed with travel permits and a military escort for protection from Apaches traveled south each January to the big trade fair in Chihuahua — a forty-day journey from Santa Fe. Some of the traders then fanned out to other towns on the northern frontier of New Spain. They returned home with trunks full of clothing, shoes, iron tools, chocolate, sugar, tobacco, paper, books, and other items that kept New Mexico in at least the backwaters of the mainstream of Spanish culture.

Connected though it was to the heartland of New Spain, eighteenth-century New Mexico was still a poor and backward place compared to other parts of Spain's empire. In *The Mapmaker's Wife,* Robert Whitaker conjures an image of the prosperous port of Guayaquil in the Spanish viceroyalty of Peru in the mid-1700s. Three forts protect the bustling town of twenty thousand. Its economy is based on a strong import/export trade. Boats arrive with luxury goods from Europe — wine, brandy, olive oil, fine silk clothing. They depart with a wealth of goods from coastal areas and the Andean valleys — timber, cotton, woolen goods, bacon, hams, cheeses, cocoa (Whitaker 2004:33).

At a time when a thriving city in colonial Peru had a population of twenty thousand, the entire province of New Mexico had a population of only thirty-four hundred (Roberts and Roberts 1946:64). While Guayaquil was generating revenues for the royal treasury, New Mexico was draining it. In his 1803 report on the state of the economy, Governor Fernando de Chacón noted that because the province was exempt from paying the sales tax, it had not contributed anything to the royal treasury since the time of the reconquest.

And it cost the treasury some fifty-five thousand pesos per year in stipends for the New Mexico missionaries, salaries for the governor and lieutenant governor, pay for the soldiers, and annuities for the allied Indian nations (Simmons 1991:171–72).

The character of those who lived in such a poor, arid, unproductive land filled with hardship and danger was bound to be different from that of those who lived in secure, productive communities with ready access to goods and services. New Mexicans, of necessity, developed a strong streak of independence and personal initiative. They were realists and people of faith. They knew how to endure.

Nowhere in the province were these character traits more manifested than in the area around Santa Cruz, northernmost of the province's principal towns and farthest from the trade centers of northern New Spain. It's no coincidence that colcha embroidery appeared there at an early date. Women in the remote communities used their ingenuity and initiative to create a regional embroidery technique that satisfied their need for something warm and beautiful and represented their determination to endure in a world where they had to make do with what they had.

Women in the north had always been self-sufficient. They defied the stereotype of the passive, docile Spanish woman. (We have only to recall the bold actions of Doña Eufemia in response to the rigors of the Oñate expedition and the tenuous San Gabriel colony.) Records in the Spanish Archives of New Mexico show that women continually exercised their rights under Spanish law and actively engaged in buying, selling, and managing property (Jenkins 1983:335). They held property in Santa Cruz as early as 1706. That year, Teresa de Herrera y Sandoval instituted legal proceedings against a couple over a debt for land. In 1731 a woman instituted proceedings against another woman, again over land. And in 1733 officials addressed the complaint of Antonia Jirón against Miguel Martín Serrano for molestation (Spanish Archives of New Mexico, Series 2, 7:183).

The tragedy of one courageous woman, who was remembered for her independence and initiative, was documented in 1941 by an interviewer working for the Federal Writers' Project (Thorp 1941). Relating the episode to the interviewer was a woman named Vicenta Sánchez, who was born in or around 1864. Her grandmother had told her the story, so we can guess that the event took place during the final decade of the eighteenth century.

The setting for her story was a small village in northern New Mexico, where it was the custom for the most able men to conduct a buffalo hunt each fall to provide the community with meat for the winter. The *ciboleros* (buffalo hunters) generally spent three or four months in the eastern grasslands hunting the animals, dressing the kill, drying the meat, and bringing back wagons full of jerky. Such expeditions were dangerous, and the community greatly admired the hunters. When the wagons left each year, everyone in town gathered to cheer the ciboleros and wish them success and safe travels. Women whose husbands remained at home were said to bow their heads in shame.

One such woman, Alvina, the mother of five children, had a lazy, worthless husband named Marcos, called Marquitos because he was small. The night before the hunters were to leave, one of the wagon drivers fell and broke his leg. The wagon boss asked Marquitos to take the driver's place, but Marquitos said he had pains in his stomach and was much too sick to go. Being a strong, resourceful woman who did most of the work for the family anyway, Alvina went to the ciboleros and begged them to take her in place of her husband. They refused at first, but the next morning the wagons pulled out of town with Alvina as one of the drivers.

Marquitos was not in the crowd of villagers that welcomed the hunting party when it returned. The men praised Alvina's work, and when the buffalo jerky was divided, she received a large share. Several days later, one of her children ran screaming to the home of a neighbor. The hysterical youngster sobbed that her mother was dead on the floor in a pool of blood. After surviving the rigors of the buffalo hunt and putting food on the family table, Alvina had been stabbed to death by her spiteful and cowardly husband. The community administered swift punishment on behalf of the woman who had demonstrated such courage. The ciboleros found Marquitos hiding in a cottonwood grove on the banks of the river and hanged him on the spot.

Although hunting supplemented the diet of many New Mexicans, the mainstay of life in Santa Cruz had always been subsistence farming and stock raising. Records show that the government distributed tools and seeds to its residents as early as 1712. Families succeeded in raising wheat, corn, beans, chili, and other vegetables. The settlers dug and maintained *acequias* (irrigation ditches) to carry water from the river to their fields. In 1732 the governor issued an order admonishing residents of Santa Cruz to take better care

View of Santa Cruz, New Mexico, around 1915. Farm fields surround the old Santa Cruz church and adjacent community in this early-twentieth-century photograph. The Sangre de Cristo Mountains are seen in the background. Courtesy Photo Archives, Palace of the Governors (MNM/DCA), Santa Fe (negative 102247).

of their livestock, which apparently was trespassing on neighboring property and causing damage that resulted in legal proceedings.

The specter of death was always present. Smallpox broke out about once a decade and took its deadly toll. Families also had to contend with marauding animals, rattlesnakes, freezing temperatures, drought, crop failures, and floods. The old church on the south side of the river, which was built prior to the Pueblo Revolt, was falling apart. In 1732 the viceroy approved the building of a new church in Santa Cruz. Before starting construction of the church, residents moved the entire settlement away from the floodplain that had brought them such misery.

Early in the century, colonists had migrated east from the Santa Cruz settlement into the upper Santa Cruz Valley. They lived in scattered homes and worked farms in the area of Chimayó (Usner 1995: 54). The mountain settlements of Las Trampas, established in 1751, and Las Truchas, established in 1754, were put in place to buffer the populous Santa Cruz Valley from Comanche raiders who came through the high country of the Sangre de Cristo Mountains (deBuys 1985:67).

Indian raids were the most persistent danger to the farming communities of northern New Mexico. Nomadic tribes — Apache, Comanche, Kiowa, Ute, Navajo — completely encircled the Pueblo Indian and Spanish settlements of the Rio Grande Valley and periodically attacked those settlements to take food, livestock, and prisoners.

The Pueblo Indians joined forces with the Spanish to defend their world against the nomadic raiders. Government records from the eighteenth century are filled with reports of hundreds of raids, orders for retaliatory campaigns, campaign reports, and attempts at peace negotiations. New Mexico seldom had more than a hundred soldiers in its standing army in the presidio in Santa Fe, so the campaigns relied heavily on local militias — squads of Pueblo Indian and Spanish farmers (Torrez 2005).

Governor Juan Bautista de Anza, a veteran Indian fighter from northern New Spain, was sent to New Mexico to help defend the beleaguered settlements. In 1779 he mustered a six-hundred-man force at Ohkay Owingeh Pueblo to wage a campaign against the forces of Green Horn, a Comanche leader whom Anza termed the scourge of the kingdom. When the governor saw the local militiamen who answered his call, he was appalled. Their scrawny, underfed horses and motley assortment of weapons were far from adequate for serious campaign duty (Simmons 1988:89).

The governor did what he could to shore up the sorry state of his volunteers. He issued each a horse and supplies, then headed north to deal with the Comanche. A clever and experienced tactician, he surprised and killed Green Horn in a successful campaign. Thereafter, the Comanche signed a treaty and became dependable allies against other tribes that plagued New Mexicans.

Although raids continued well into the nineteenth century, there was a measure of peace in the land by the end of the eighteenth century. Folk art was on the rise in a culture that had become uniquely New Mexican. Members of the new culture, although poor, were resilient and innovative. In the northern part of the province, a distinctive embroidery technique had emerged. Women embraced the new technique. It was a satisfying way for them to express their love for their families and their faith.

Santa Cruz grew from 1,301 inhabitants in 1789 to 10,185 in 1793 (Jones 1979:243). As the population increased, independence and initiative impelled many to move away from the towns to less populated sites. As early as 1724, Cristóval de Torres of Santa Cruz had petitioned the governor for land in Chama, some seventy miles to the north (Spanish Archives of New Mexico, Series 2, 21:289). Families from the Santa Cruz Valley continued to migrate to outlying areas. And when they relocated to new settlements, they took along the practice and images of colcha embroidery.

Colorful embroidery that includes the couching stitch embellishes a bodice made in the Andalusia region of Spain in the early eighteenth century. Photo by Dave Benson.

CHAPTER 3

1800s: Heyday of the Needle Art

The practice of colcha embroidery reached its prime during the first half of the nineteenth century, maturing from adolescence into full-blown adulthood. Women in the remote regions of northern New Mexico had developed and perpetuated a technique of embroidery all their own — a style based on just one traditional stitch. Well into the nineteenth century, they continued to embroider almost exclusively in the colcha stitch.

Why did they limit themselves to just one stitch? Experienced needleworkers speculate that Hispanic women in the northern Rio Grande Valley preferred this technique because colcha is an easy and extremely flexible stitch. With the colcha stitch, the homemaker could cover a large area of sabanilla more quickly than with any other stitch.

Couched (colcha) stitches appeared in embroidery done in Spain and New Spain, but generally in combination with other types of stitches. A bodice made in Spain during the first half of the eighteenth century includes couched stitches and satin stitches done in silk thread. Samplers embroidered in New Spain during the late eighteenth century feature couched threads of silver plus various colors of silk thread worked in satin stitches, stem stitches, and French knots.

Using silver thread and large quantities of fine silk floss was not an option for women in the settlements around Santa Cruz. Far from the mainstream of trade, families in the northern farming communities had limited access to luxury products and were not a ready market for extravagance.

The struggle to eke out a living by farming and raising livestock was still a way of life in the northern communities at the beginning of the nineteenth century. The general lack of prosperity in New Mexico was documented by one of its more prosperous residents, sixty-year-old Pedro Bautista Pino, in a fifty-one-page report. The gentleman was the province's representative to the *cortes* (parliament) in Spain, and in 1812 he made the ten-month trip from Santa Fe to Cádiz at his own expense to deliver his report.

Pino urged the government of Spain to help fix the stagnant economy of New Mexico. One of the most pressing problems was the unfavorable balance of trade with unscrupulous merchants in Chihuahua, who took advantage of their monopoly under Spanish law. Pino also asked for support for the province's overburdened militia; hostile Indians continued to raid settlements and steal livestock, and Anglo-Americans were an increasingly threatening presence at the borders. There were only twenty-two Franciscan friars and two secular priests to serve a population of forty thousand residents in the province's four villas, twenty-six pueblos, and 102 scattered defensive plazas (Kessell 2002:359).

One such defensive plaza was the settlement of Chimayó, eight miles up the road from Santa Cruz. A record shows that women there were busy embroidering in 1818. The inventory of the Santuario de Esquipulas includes a length of five varas of *sábana de sabanilla labrada* (embroidered handwoven wool; probably an altar cloth) and a new colcha (Minge 1979: 20). Other items in the inventory were of a kind and quantity that led Boyd to conclude that they weren't just for use in the chapel. Her theory is that Don Bernardo Abeitia, donor-builder of the chapel, hired local weavers and needleworkers to make goods to be sold on site to bring in funds for the maintenance of the building. She noted an unusual architectural feature — two rooms built against the facade of the chapel. They were probably storage and salesrooms where pilgrims and visitors could purchase embroideries and other shop goods (Boyd 1974:68 – 70).

The style of colcha embroidery that the women of Chimayó did for Don Abeitia's salesrooms came to be termed wool-on-wool. For materials, they used hand-spun, home-dyed yarn and a ground of loosely woven sabanilla. They completely covered the sabanilla with colcha stitches. Some stitches formed the design elements, and the rest filled the background (negative space) around the designs.

The wool-on-wool style uses lots of yarn. But even the poorest of households could afford a lot of yarn. Sheep were plentiful, so wool was low in value. In 1810 the Anglo-American soldier-adventurer Zebulon Pike reported that merchants in northern New Spain sold high-quality, imported textiles for the equivalent of twenty-five dollars per yard, whereas New Mexico sheep sold for just one dollar a head (Simmons 1988:99).

The old wool-on-wool colchas were made from the fleece of churro sheep. The fleece of the churro is low in lanolin (grease), so it needs less washing than the fleece of other breeds. The wool has long, straight fibers that are relatively easy to clean, spin, and dye. The women used a single-ply yarn for the embroidery. They generally finished the edges of their work with a simple yarn fringe.

The procedure for producing the yarn may have varied somewhat from village to village and family to family. But the overall process of converting a raw fleece to finished yarn was long and laborious, no matter how it was accomplished. Rita Padilla Haufmann, who weaves traditional Rio Grande textiles today, describes the process she has developed to wash, card, and spin her yarn. Her process combines traditional and decidedly modern techniques.

First she selects a fleece for its cleanliness, color, luster, and length of fiber. Then she scours (washes) the fleece, soaking it for a long period in hot water to remove the natural grease and dirt. Next she rinses the fleece and lets it dry slowly. As it dries, she separates (teases) the fibers to speed up the drying and to prepare them for carding. When the fibers are dry, she cards the wool, drawing it through parallel rows of metal teeth to align the fibers into soft mats that are ready for spinning. Using a foot-powered spinning wheel, she spins the fluffy mats into twisted yarn. Then she winds the yarn into skeins and again washes and rinses it. In the final rinse she includes a few drops of pennyroyal oil to discourage moths. Finally, she dries the skeins under tension to set the twist. At this point, the yarn is ready to be dyed.

Haufmann uses the natural light and dark tones of the fleece in her weaving, as well as yarn she colors with vegetal dyes traditionally used by New Mexicans. She produces yellows from several native plants—snakeweed, canaigre, Indian paintbrush, and chamisa. Cota, another native plant, yields oranges and rusts. Madder, a root, yields corals. She uses imported indigo for blue, logwood for purple, brazilwood for a deep rose, and cochineal — a tiny bug that grows on cacti in Mexico — for reds and magentas.

Yarn spun and dyed by northern New Mexico weaver Rita Padilla Haufmann. Photo by Dave Benson.

Extracting the dyes from their sources and fixing them onto the spun yarn involves several steps. First Haufmann simmers the skeins in a bath of mordants (alum and cream of tartar) to prepare the yarn to accept and hold the color. Then she steeps and brews the dyestuff to produce the dye liquor. When the dye liquor is ready, she simmers the skeins in the dye bath in an outdoor solar oven for about a day — a slow process at low temperatures that yields rich, vibrant colors. By adding or removing skeins of yarn at different times during the dye bath, she can produce a range of related hues from one dye pot. She hangs the skeins to dry, then washes and rinses them one more time. When the skeins are completely dry, the yarn is ready to be used.

Haufmann has a strong interest in, and connection to, New Mexican women of the past. She discovered that two of her ancestral grandmothers were listed as stocking knitters in the 1823 census for Rio de Tesuque, the village north of Santa Fe where she grew up and lives today with her husband, son, and relatives. As far back as the 1660s, Governor Bernardo López de Mendizábal had women make stockings that he exported with other local goods to markets in the mining communities of northern New Spain (Scholes 1937:390).

In thinking about those New Mexicans of the past who worked with wool, and in experiencing for herself the large amount of work involved in spinning and dyeing that wool, Haufmann came up with an interesting theory. She believes that not every homemaker who did colcha embroidery spent time making the embroidery yarn from scratch. Some probably obtained and used ends of dyed yarn that were left over from weaving colorful Rio Grande textiles — the blankets, serapes, and *jerga* (a multipurpose twill yardage, used primarily for floor covering) that played such an important role in the trade and economy of the province. She speculates that nothing went to waste. Those ends of yarn were of no further use to the weaver, but they were a gold mine of colors that women could use to add beauty and interest to their needlework.

Several points support her theory. First, we know that weavers worked in Santa Cruz and other towns in the province in the early nineteenth century. An 1822 inventory of looms in New Mexico indicates that Santa Cruz had fourteen. Albuquerque, which had more sheep because of ample pastureland and better access to water, had seventy-one looms (Minge 1979:27). There's also an observation made by Marianne Stoller, an anthropologist who studied the Hispanic arts and crafts of her native San Luis Valley in southern Colorado. She remarks that the colors that appear in early colcha embroideries are the same ones used in weaving (Stoller 1977:87).

Wool-on-Wool Colchas

The ground of all the wool-on-wool colchas was sabanilla — a white, wool sheeting produced on treadle looms. Sabanilla, the diminutive in Spanish of *sábana* (sheet), is a balanced plain-weave fabric. In this type of weave, the fabric has the same number of warp (lengthwise) threads as weft (horizontal) threads. The warp threads, which are made of the

same yarn as the weft, are exposed rather than covered completely by the weft threads. The churro fleece has a hairy outer coat and a soft inner one. Generally, the yarn found in the sabanilla used for colcha embroidery contains a relatively high proportion of hair (outer coat) fibers.

The typical sabanilla was about thirty inches wide and had some twelve to twenty-two threads to the inch (Fisher 1979:155). It was considerably finer than other yardage produced on New Mexico looms. Before embroidering on it, women would sew together three widths to make a ground that was large enough to cover a bed or an altar. They left the sides (selvages) intact, and turned and hemmed both ends of the sabanilla before beginning to embroider.

There are few remaining examples of the old wool-on-wool colchas. In 1978 the Museum of International Folk Art (MOIFA) in Santa Fe completed a comprehensive survey of Rio Grande Spanish textiles in the collections of forty institutions across the United States. Of the two thousand textiles identified and analyzed, there were fewer than twenty wool-on-wool colcha embroideries. Survey director Nora Fisher, curator of textiles at MOIFA, concluded that the wool-on-wool embroideries probably all came from the northern Rio Grande Valley (Fisher 1979:162). It's difficult to hazard a guess as to how many of the old wool-on-wool colchas were actually produced. Over the years, they may have simply worn out from continued use and been discarded, or been deemed too old-fashioned to bother keeping.

Fisher identified several probable sources of the designs found on the wool-on-wool colchas examined in the survey: the title page of the Carmelite book of accounts in the Santa Cruz church, textiles from New Spain, and textiles from the Manila galleon trade (Fisher 1979:158–62). The Manila galleon trade had been bringing textiles with elaborate, curvilinear floral patterns to New Spain since the middle of the 1500s. In the seventeenth and eighteenth centuries, the textiles were exported in large quantities from the southeastern coast of India to markets all over the world, in complex interactions of trade among India, Europe, and East Asia. Termed *indianas* or *indianillas* (Indian chintz or calico), this hand-painted or -printed cotton cloth was widely used in New Spain, particularly for clothing, and was an important design source for embroidery.

Opposite: Wool-on-wool colcha, 1790–1850. Photo by Blair Clark. Courtesy Fred Harvey Fine Arts Collection. International Folk Art Foundation Collection at the Museum of International Folk Art (DCA), Santa Fe (FA.79.64-94).

The Arabesque Motif

The meandering vine tying together floral and leaf elements in the early colchas is an image that predates seventeenth-century Indian chintz and Chinese silks. A fragment of embroidery from a Viking barrow burial in Denmark depicts a vine with associated images (Staniland 1991:5). Some textile historians believe that patterns based on plants were used even before the coming of Islam in the seventh century.

Islamic dynasties had ruled the southern Iberian Peninsula for nearly seven hundred years by the time the Catholic monarchs of Spain ousted the last ruler of Muslim Andalusia in 1492. During the sixteenth century in Spain, Islamic imagery remained a strong influence. The religious and secular art of Islam was limited to calligraphics, geometrics, and plant-based ornament. The foliate scroll design that covers much of the surface of Islamic art—curling stems set with abstract leaf and geometric motifs—is still referred to as arabesque.

It's tempting to assume that individuals who went to New Spain—especially those from the central and southern parts of the Iberian Peninsula—took along cherished items embroidered with intricate arabesques and other images from what had been Muslim Andalusia. We know that the earliest professional embroidery guilds in Mexico City conducted examinations for proficiency in executing arabesque patterns (Toussaint 1967:71).

There is little doubt that this popular and easily transported textile eventually wound up in New Mexico and inspired the designs found on many early colchas. The colchas exhibit graceful, free-flowing patterns composed of hybrid, stylized flowers, disembodied C-shaped forms, and leaves that intertwine with, and are vaguely attached to, meandering vines. The same motifs and designs characterize Indian chintz. The Manila galleons also brought large quantities of fine silk embroideries from China. The delicate scroll-shaped leaves and flowers stitched on the silk may also have inspired colcha designs.

Our modern, consumer-oriented culture puts far less value on textiles than people did in the past. We take for granted that we can fill our closets with mass-produced clothing of every size and color from stores and online catalogs. When we tire of an item, we simply discard it. But centuries ago, clothing and furnishings were rare and valuable items. Families at every level of society treasured them, willed them to their

Opposite: Wool-on-wool colcha, 1750–1825. Photo by Blair Clark. Courtesy Museum of New Mexico Collection at the Museum of International Folk Art (DCA), Santa Fe (FA.5.54.9).

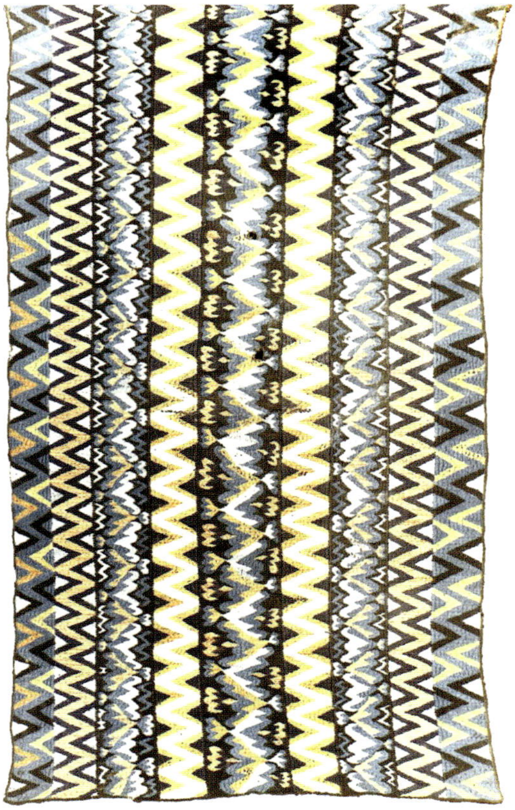

Wool-on-wool colcha, New Mexico, 1850–1870. Collected by James L. Seligman. Photo by Saskia Kesners. Colorado Springs Fine Arts Center, Taylor Museum, Colorado Springs. Gift of Alice Bemis Taylor (TM 3775).

Opposite: Wool-on-wool colcha, 1800–1850. Acquired in the San Luis Valley of southern Colorado. Courtesy Museum of Spanish Colonial Art, Collections of the Spanish Colonial Arts Society, Inc., Santa Fe, New Mexico. Gift of Mary Cabot Wheelwright (1958.041).

heirs, and even traded prized items for staples in times of need.

It's not difficult to imagine that a beautifully embroidered silk shawl inherited from a well-to-do relative would be included with the belongings of a woman who made the long trip across the ocean to New Spain, and then up the Rio Grande to northern New Mexico. That woman later willed her daughter the treasured heirloom from the Old World. Over the decades, the patterns in that same shawl may have percolated through the farming communities around Santa Cruz and been reinvested with vitality by a creative homemaker.

Wool-on-Cotton Colchas

In 1821 there occurred a political change that had a great impact on the colcha embroidery tradition — as it did on every other aspect of life in the province of New Mexico. New Spain threw off Spanish rule and declared itself an independent nation, as did many other parts of Spanish America at that time. After 223 years as subjects of the king of Spain, New Mexicans found themselves citizens of the new nation of Mexico. Although Santa Cruz and the other towns of New Mexico had taken no direct part in the revolution against Spain, they welcomed the new flag because Mexican officials abolished Spain's monopoly on commerce and restrictions on travel.

Now that they could legally conduct business in the former lands of Spain, traders from the United States took full advantage of the opportunity. They began sending caravans laden with thousands of pounds of goods to New Mexico. Santa Fe became the primary trade center of the region. In 1843 some half-million dollars in goods flowed into town (Roberts and Roberts 1946:92). The caravans that plied their way from Missouri to Santa Fe traveled across what came to be known as the Santa Fe Trail.

When traders from the United States arrived in 1821 with tightly woven, factory-made cotton yardage and finer plied yarns, the old embroidery tradition developed a separate but parallel branch. Many women in New Mexico added what came to be termed the wool-on-cotton style of colcha embroidery to their repertoires. The 1978 MOIFA survey of Rio Grande Spanish textiles in the collections of forty institutions across the United States found and studied more than fifty wool-on-cotton colchas. Project director Nora Fisher believes that essentially all those colchas were made in northern New Mexico (Fisher 1979:165).

Cotton fabric had been a rare commodity in New Mexico prior to the opening of the Santa Fe Trail trade route. Imported cotton cloth from England had been available at trade fairs in northern New Spain, but few could afford the expensive material. Shortly after the traders arrived, the market was flooded with commercial yarn and a tempting assortment of affordable, factory-made yardage: cotton twill, printed cotton (calico, gingham), linen, silk, fine woolens, flannel, bayeta, serge, taffeta, velvet.

Women began to experiment with embroidering on the inexpensive new yardage — usually twill — rather than on sabanilla. The thick, hand-spun, single-ply yarn they had used in the past was ideal for embroidering on the loosely woven sabanilla, but it frayed when used on the tightly woven, factory-made yardage. As a result, women used the traders' thin, plied commercial yarn for embroidering on the new commercial fabric.

This change in materials in the new branch of colcha embroidery resulted in a change in design. With the finer embroidery yarns on the tightly woven yardage, it was far more difficult and time-consuming to completely cover the ground fabric with stitches. Consequently, women began stitching isolated, freestanding motifs rather than covering the entire ground with a continuum of stitches as they did in the wool-on-wool style. Those freestanding design elements became a distinguishing feature of the wool-on-cotton branch of colcha embroidery.

Although the New Mexico needlework tradition had added the wool-on-cotton branch, the colcha stitch was still fundamental to, and dominant in, the embroidery. Additional types of stitches — chain, stem, satin, and split stitches—appeared in the wool-on-cotton work. Many of the designs, as well as the stitches, found on the wool-on-cotton colchas reflect the influence of Anglo-American crewel embroidery. The new, freestanding designs included small birds, insects, and the elaborate flower motifs characteristic of crewel embroidery. New Mexico women also began to create designs based on their own surroundings — pronghorn antelope, deer, and even buffalo, the latter of which appears in a colcha made in the mid-nineteenth century (see page 76).

Some of the colchas featured a large central motif — a medallion or floral bouquet — surrounded by smaller, repeated elements. They often had an outer border of flowers, as well as distinctive corner elements. Bedspreads embroidered in Spain and Mexico had similar central motifs and corner elements and may have been prototypes for early New Mexico wool-on-cotton embroideries.

Wool-on-cotton colcha, New Mexico, mid- to late 1800s. Collected by Governor Arthur Seligman. Photo by Saskia Kesners. Colorado Springs Fine Arts Center, Taylor Museum, Colorado Springs. Gift of Alice Bemis Taylor (TM 3790).

The Impact of Indian Chintz Designs

The dominant design source for both the wool-on-wool and wool-on-cotton colchas was Indian chintz. The influential designs took two different routes to New Mexico, traveling across two different oceans in the course of two different centuries. The fabric first crossed the Pacific in the holds of the Manila galleons during the seventeenth century, spread throughout New Spain, and then spread north to New Mexico.

A second wave of Indian chintz designs arrived in New Mexico during the nineteenth century, having previously crossed the Atlantic Ocean from England. The quasi-realistic, hybrid floral designs had been wildly popular in England during the seventeenth and eighteenth centuries. Large quantities of the fabric were sold to customers in England who craved exotic goods. The Indian textile manufacturers combined elements of Islamic art, Persian and Ottoman carpets, and Chinese ceramics in their designs.

Over decades of trade, designs that traveled back and forth between England and India were modified to cater to market taste. Some Indian chintz patterns evolved into faithful renditions of English crewel embroidery—a practice dating to late-seventeenth-century England in which stitching was done in brightly colored worsted wool yarn on wall and bed hangings. The continually modified designs traveled to the eastern seaboard of the United States with colonists from England. Their descendants—wives of Anglo-American traders, soldiers, and merchants—brought these designs with them when they migrated down the Santa Fe Trail to New Mexico in the early nineteenth century.

Opposite top: Wool-on-cotton colcha, New Mexico, mid- to late 1800s. Collected by James L. Seligman. Photo by Saskia Kesners. Courtesy Colorado Springs Fine Arts Center, Taylor Museum, Colorado Springs. Gift of Alice Bemis Taylor (TM 3780).

Opposite bottom: Wool-on-cotton colcha, New Mexico, mid-1800s. Courtesy Museum of Spanish Colonial Art, Collections of the Spanish Colonial Arts Society, Inc., Santa Fe. Gift of Gustave Pabst (1957.36).

Wool-on-cotton colcha, New Mexico, mid- to late 1800s. Collected by James L. Seligman. Photo by Saskia Kesners. Colorado Springs Fine Arts Center, Taylor Museum, Colorado Springs. Gift of Alice Bemis Taylor (TM 3784).

Wool-on-cotton colcha, New Mexico, mid- to late 1800s. Collected by Governor Arthur Seligman. Photo by Saskia Kesners. Courtesy Colorado Springs Fine Arts Center, Taylor Museum, Colorado Springs. Gift of Alice Bemis Taylor (TM 3789).

Above: Wool-on-cotton colcha depicting buffalo, which New Mexicans hunted for their hides and meat. Abiquiu, New Mexico, about 1870. Collected by H. H. Garnett. Photo by Saskia Kesners. Courtesy Colorado Springs Fine Arts Center, Taylor Museum, Colorado Springs. Gift of Alice Bemis Taylor (TM 3785).

Right: Pronghorn antelope, which still populate the plains of northern New Mexico, appear as a motif in New Mexico Colonial Embroidery in an instruction booklet published by the New Mexico Department of Vocational Education and Training in 1935.

Opposite: Embroidered bedspread, Spain, late eighteenth or early nineteenth century. Courtesy Museum of Spanish Colonial Art, Collections of the Spanish Colonial Arts Society, Inc., Santa Fe (1981.3).

Embroidered bedspread, Mexico, mid-nineteenth century. Courtesy Museum of Spanish Colonial Art, Collections of the Spanish Colonial Arts Society, Inc., Santa Fe (1980.1).

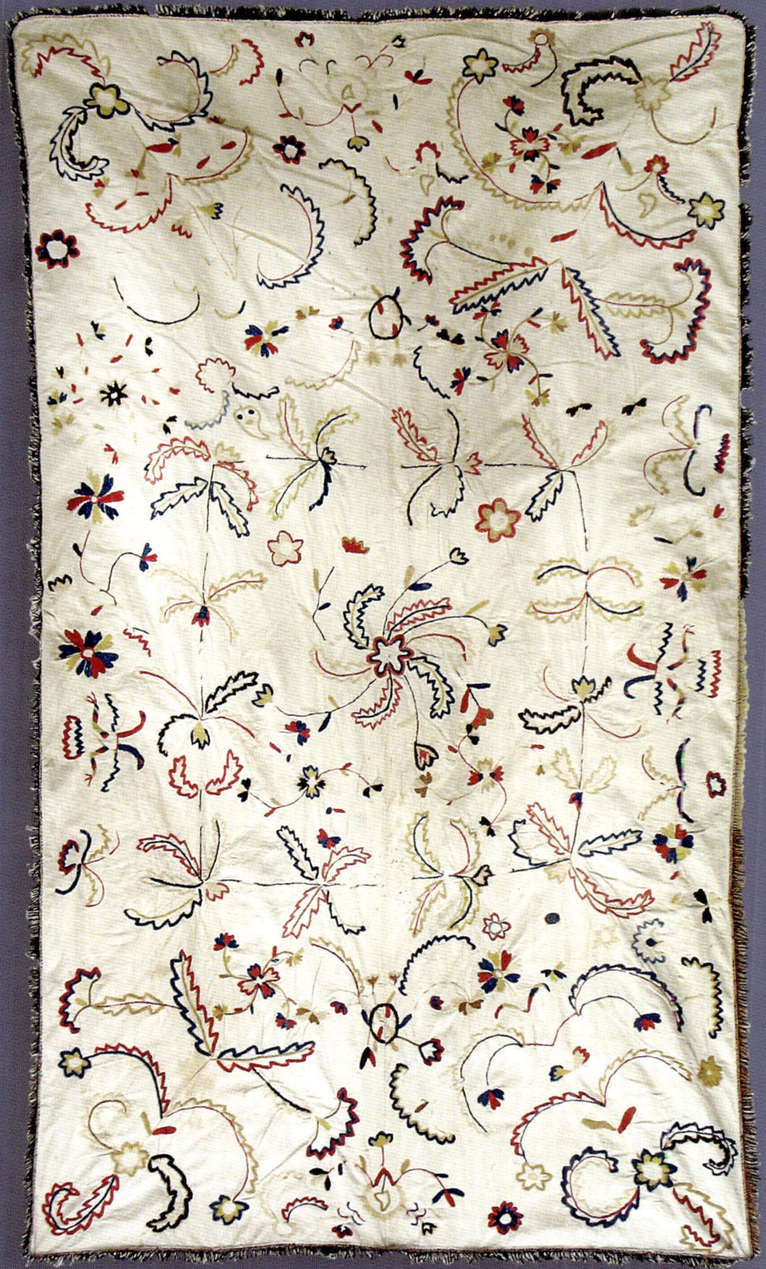

This embroidered wool-on-cotton bedspread, made in New Mexico in the mid- to late 1800s, includes the colcha stitch. With its floral patterns, central motif enclosed in a rectangle, distinctive corner elements, and fringe, it is related in style to bedspreads made in Spain and Mexico. Collected by James L. Seligman. Photo by Saskia Kesners. Courtesy Colorado Springs Fine Arts Center, Taylor Museum, Colorado Springs. Gift of Alice Bemis Taylor (TM 3778).

New Mexico Colchas as Items of Commerce

Like the Anglo-American traders, New Mexicans wasted little time in taking advantage of the new political situation in 1821. Mexican officials taxed trade items that arrived from the United States, but items that were made or grown in New Mexico — *efectos del país* — were allowed to move duty-free to markets in the south. New Mexican merchants armed themselves, joined together in convoys for mutual protection, and headed to the interior of Mexico.

It was forty days of travel from Santa Fe to Chihuahua, the city most frequently registered as the destination for the caravans (Boyle 1997:36). Women sometimes accompanied men on the trading trips. Between 1835 and 1845, some five hundred New Mexicans loaded sturdy pack mules and ox carts with bundles of handmade articles and local goods destined for Mexico — buffalo hides, salt, piñon nuts, and the colorful handwoven textiles that New Mexicans had been producing for more than two centuries.

Trade manifests indicate that not only were colchas being produced for this commerce, they were generally the highest-value items in the shipments. We can speculate that these colchas were both wool-on-wool and wool-on-cotton. *Guías* (traders' passports that often included cargo lists) provide a snapshot of the level of production and status of colcha embroideries during this peak period of textile export, which lasted until the United States declared war on Mexico in 1846.

Examining the guías preserved in the Mexican Archives of New Mexico, historian Ward Alan Minge came up with numbers of colchas shipped to Mexico during three years: 111 in 1838, 47 in 1840, and 153 in 1844 (Minge 1979:26). Many guías include only a single colcha. But one in 1838 includes eighteen. A shipment in 1840 includes thirteen, and one in 1844 includes thirty.

The guías show that the colchas were high-value items. Based on a calculation for eleven guías selected at random from the period 1838 to 1845, the average value of a colcha was three pesos. Buffalo hides were generally valued at one peso. Ordinary woven blankets ranged from two reales to one peso (one peso equaled eight reales). Most serapes ranged from two reales to two pesos. Colchas ranged from two to as much as thirteen pesos, although the thirteen-peso value cannot be considered representative and was not included in the average-value calculation. The 1840 shipment in which the thirteen-peso colcha appears lists consistently inflated values.

The guías provide disappointingly few details about the colchas, but the textiles must have been decorated with appealing embroidery in order to command consistently high prices. One guía for a shipment in 1838 includes *una colcha bordada con lana de Castilla* (one colcha embroidered with Castilian wool) (Mexican Archives of New Mexico 25:439). Textile scholar Josie Caruso believes that this colcha, destined for market in Chihuahua or Sonora, was quite likely wool-on-cotton. The Castilian wool was probably a plied commercial yarn made from the fleece of merino sheep and exported to New Mexico over the Santa Fe Trail.

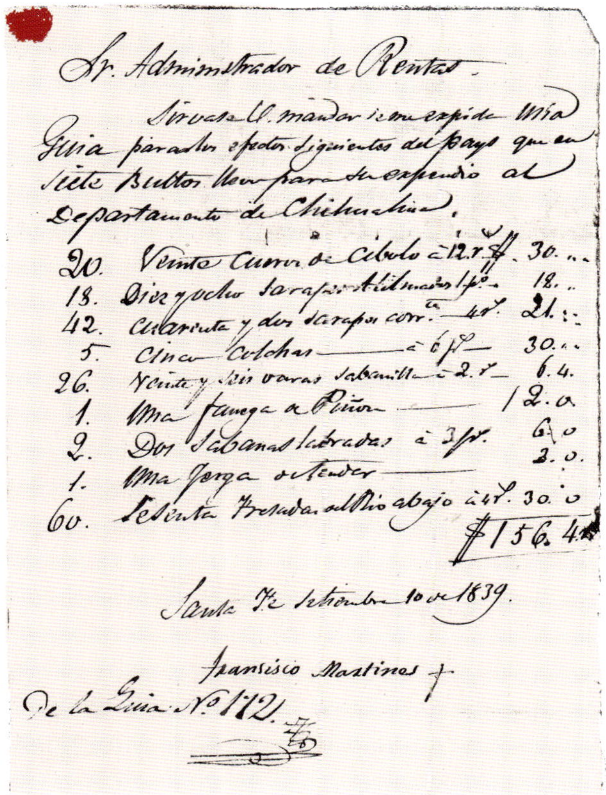
Sr. Administrador de Rentas.
Sirvase U. mandar se me expida una Guia para los efectos siguientes del Pays que en siete Bultos llevo para su expendio al Departamento de Chihuahua.
20. Veinte Cueros de Cibolo a 12 r. [illegible] 30.
18. Diez y ocho sarapes [illegible] 18.
42. Cuarenta y dos sarapes corr. [illegible] 21.
5. Cinco colchas a 6 p. 30.
26. Veinte y seis varas sabanilla a 2 r. 6.4.
1. Una fanega de Piñon 12.0
2. Dos Sabanas labradas a 3 p. 6.0
1. Una Jerga [illegible] 3.0
60. Sesenta Frezadas del Rio abajo a 4 r. 30.0
$156.4
Santa Fe Setiembre 10 de 1839.
Francisco Martines
De la Guia No. 172.

A list of goods showing that textiles embroidered in New Mexico (colchas and sábanas labradas) were high-value export items in the mid-1800s. Courtesy New Mexico State Records Center and Archives (MANM reel 27: frame 624).

A shipment destined for Chihuahua in 1839 included two different types of embroidered items — five colchas valued at six pesos each and two *sábanas labradas* (embroidered sheets) valued at three pesos each. Caruso speculates that the five colchas in the shipment were bedspreads, and the two sábanas labradas were altar cloths.

Records of legal proceedings and estate inventories support the finding that colchas were high-value items in the first half of the nineteenth century. The 1827 listing of the estate of a wealthy Taos rancher, Don Severino

Wool-on-cotton colcha, circa 1850, said to have been used as an altar cloth in the Cristo Rey Church, Santa Fe. Courtesy Museum of Spanish Colonial Art, Collections of the Spanish Colonial Arts Society, Inc., Santa Fe (1973.011).

Opposite: Wool-on-cotton colcha, circa 1865, made for a family chapel near Peñasco, New Mexico. Photo by Blair Clark. Courtesy Museum of New Mexico Collection at the Museum of International Folk Art (DCA), Santa Fe (A.67.44.1).

Martínez, included a colcha appraised at six pesos. In 1822 a merchant named Pedro Armendaris had his goods impounded in Santa Fe for neglecting to pay taxes on trade with Chihuahua for the previous three years. The inventory of his merchandise included eighteen locally produced colchas valued at eight pesos each. He also had 398 varas of sabanilla and 12,100 imported sewing needles (Minge 1979:24).

The Parallel Practices of Wool-on-Wool and Wool-on-Cotton Embroidery

Through the balance of the nineteenth century, descendants of the Spanish colonists in northern New Mexico continued to make wool-on-wool colchas, which they embroidered with both homemade and commercial yarn. Homemakers had an ample supply of the yarn and sabanilla they needed to continue embroidering in the wool-on-wool style. The census shows that weavers in the town of Abiquiu, north of Santa Cruz, were still making sabanilla in 1829; the cloth had a value of one to two reales per vara (Minge 1979:27). And there was no dearth of wool. The 1822 census indicates that there were 2,816 sheep in Santa Cruz (23).

Women continued to embroider altar cloths for churches and family chapels. They still embellished their bedspreads with colorful designs that added beauty to their homes. They even began embroidering on fabric cut to the size and shape of curtains (*cortinas labradas*), which they used as covers for the new glazed windows that traders brought from the East.

The traditional wool-on-wool style had branched early in the century to include the wool-on-cotton style, with its

factory-made fabric and yarn, freestanding designs, and additional types of stitches. Not everyone bought and used the new commercial yarn. Some families continued to make their own. They used the fleece of the churro for this purpose until about 1860, when commercial breeders from the East introduced the merino and other breeds that yielded more profit — more wool per shearing and more meat. But the oily, crimped fleece of the new breeds was much harder to clean, spin, and dye. The wool spun into a lumpy yarn that was inferior to the smooth strands of the churro. By the end of the century, when the characteristics of the new breeds had effectively contaminated the churro stock, the texture of handmade yarn was of such poor quality that few families continued to produce it.

Just a few decades after Spain's trade monopoly was lifted and New Mexicans were beginning to incorporate an unprecedented bounty of new products into their daily lives, the United States declared war on Mexico. In 1848 a defeated Mexico ceded territory comprising modern-day Texas, California, New Mexico, Arizona, and southern Utah to the land-hungry young republic. Having been citizens of Mexico for just twenty-five years, the descendants of the Spanish settlers who colonized the remote frontiers of New Spain found themselves citizens of the United States of America. Under the new flag, they had access to an even wider range of manufactured yardage and clothing and a far larger variety of trade goods.

Thanks to an interview conducted by the Federal Writers' Project in 1941, we can reach back to the year 1870 and listen to a firsthand account of women working on their embroidery. The same Vicenta Sánchez who related her grandmother's story about the woman who went on a buffalo hunt (see chapter 2) described her memories of learning colcha embroidery as a six-year-old girl in the Spanish village of Pena Blanca, near Santa Fe.

Vicenta said that her aunt sewed very well and earned money making colcha bedspreads for those who could afford to buy them. She embroidered on flannel and unbleached muslin, which were brought in by wagon trains from the East. Her aunt drew patterns of birds and flowers in charcoal on the ground fabric. She embroidered the designs with wool dyed with native dyes, then spun very fine (Thorp 1941).

It was her aunt and her grandmother who taught the young girls of the household how to sew. Vicenta recalls that they did most of the sewing at night, by the light of the fireplace. She and the other girls were given ravelings and scraps of cloth to practice their stitching. Using the recycled materials, the girls embroidered pretty *colchitas,* little bedspreads, for their dolls. Vicenta explained that the girls practiced with ravelings because thread was very expensive in those days — as much as twenty-five cents a spool. They were motivated by their grandmother's promise that when they learned to sew neatly, they would be given better materials. Then they would be able to embroider real colchas, just like their aunt.

Although she didn't know it at the time, the young girl would never have the opportunity to earn money making and selling colcha bedspreads. In 1878, the year she turned fourteen, the railroad arrived in New Mexico. With the trains came a flood of goods from the East that would seriously derail the practice and desirability of colcha embroidery.

CHAPTER 4
Early 1900s: A Thread on the Verge of Breaking

The practice of colcha embroidery declined precipitously in the final years of the nineteenth century as railroads brought an influx of immigrants and new products to what was now the southwestern United States. The tenuous thread of New Mexico's Spanish colonial embroidery tradition was dangerously frayed.

By the turn of the twentieth century, trade goods had essentially replaced local weaving and regional dress in most parts of New Mexico. Even in the rural San Luis Valley of southern Colorado, a geographically isolated area that had been settled by Hispanic New Mexicans during the second half of the nineteenth century, the change effected by access to modern, machine-made products was evident.

When Marianne Stoller interviewed long-term residents of her native San Luis Valley in the 1970s, she learned that commercially woven cloth that arrived with the railroad had rapidly replaced handwoven material for clothing. Although a few of the older women still wore *tápalos* (shawls) of handwoven wool as late as the 1930s, the amount of weaving declined drastically with the advent of increasingly cheap, accessible, and admired commercial cloth (Stoller 1979:50).

As commercial cloth became more and more desirable, handwoven textiles became much less so. Woven wool textiles became increasingly coarse and bulky due to changes in fleece that occurred when Anglos introduced more profitable breeds of sheep. One long-term resident remembered that wearing a shirt made of this harsh and prickly hand-spun wool was tantamount to an act of penance.

Stoller's inquiries about the practice of colcha embroidery in the San Luis Valley elicited few memories of it. She concluded that the old colchas were gone, and probably had been since at least the turn of the century. Women she interviewed either did not recall them or knew about them only from books and museums (Stoller 1977:87 – 88).

The New Mexico Spanish colonial arts authority E. Boyd offered a bleak assessment of the state of colcha embroidery after so many homemakers had succumbed to the lure of new products and techniques. She wrote that stitchery declined in quality, as did the planning of patterns, "which grew helter-skelter as whimsical inscriptions, animals, and symbols in gaudy colors replaced handsome older designs." Her dire conclusion was that by the end of the nineteenth century, crochet, patchwork, feather stitching, and prestamped patterns for cross-stitch had literally stifled the tradition of freehand colcha embroidery (Boyd 1974:218).

As a devotee of the traditional arts and crafts of New Mexico, Boyd made no effort to hide her scorn for the outside influences that she blamed for the decline of fine embroidery. She termed the new designs and color combinations "meretricious" and pointed an angry finger at the peddlers — French, German, Polish, and Syrian — who sold Saxony and Germantown yarns and packets of aniline dyes to New Mexicans (Boyd 1974:214).

There is scant evidence that women were still doing colcha embroidery at the turn of the century. The Museum of Spanish Colonial Art in Santa Fe does have two embroideries made between 1900 and 1910, and those textiles testify to the precarious state of the old New Mexico embroidery tradition. The ground fabric is cotton flour sacking. The rough embroidery was done with aniline-dyed, plied commercial knitting yarn. The colchas are solidly embroidered with a stark, geometric design.

Opposite: Wool-on-cotton, solidly embroidered colcha (and reverse side), made at the turn of the twentieth century in northern New Mexico. Courtesy Museum of Spanish Colonial Art, Collections of the Spanish Colonial Arts Society, Inc., Santa Fe (1960.5).

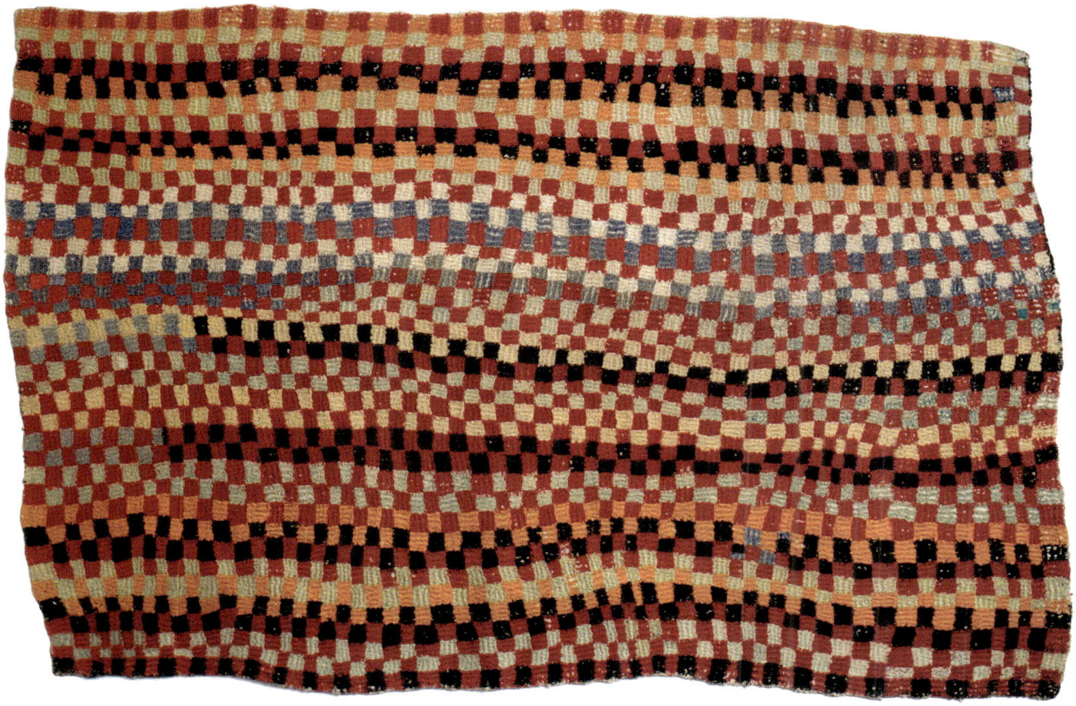

Trampas, NM. Photo by John C. Collier Jr., 1943. A homemaker spins coarse, bulky yarn by hand in a mountain village in northern New Mexico. Courtesy New Mexico Museum of Art. New Mexico Farm Security Administration, museum purchase with funds from the Pinewood Foundation, with additional support from Barbara Erdman, 1990 (1990.70.236).

Another example in the museum collection — a wool-on-wool-style textile from the turn of the twentieth century — was done with commercial knitting yarn in plain, long stitches. But the stitches lack the traditional couching (overlay) element of colcha embroidery. The ground of plain-weave homespun had been worn and patched before being embroidered. The patches are scraps of sabanilla, jerga, and machine-made, knitted underwear. In some rural home in the mountains of northern New Mexico, a homemaker was still using the materials she had at hand to make a wool bedcover even warmer by covering it with solid embroidery.

The only other evidence found to date that women were still doing colcha embroidery at the beginning of the twentieth century is anecdotal. In a newspaper article written in 1987, Eloisa Maestas, a lifelong resident of Santa Cruz, claimed that she remembers watching her aunt work on colcha embroidery when she was about seven years old (Morgan 1987:D3). Maestas would have been seven in 1908.

Although the thread of the colcha embroidery tradition was dangerously frayed at this point, it never did break — largely because most New Mexicans succeeded in resisting assimilation into the mainstream of American life for several more decades. Until the 1940s, descendants of the Spanish colonists constituted a majority of the state's population. They successfully repulsed attempts to make them give up their language, their folkways, and their traditional style of life (Simmons 1988:164).

When the other Spanish-speaking provinces that the United States had acquired from Mexico in 1848 became states of the Union, their original inhabitants soon found themselves outnumbered by Anglo-Americans. In stark contrast, Spanish-speaking people constituted a majority of New Mexico's population until the 1940s, and they succeeded in keeping the framework of Spanish culture intact. Although New Mexico became a territory of the United States in 1850, it took five unsuccessful attempts before it finally became a state in 1912.

Seventeen years before New Mexico became a state, a girl was born in the village of El Guique, near the spot where three centuries earlier, Juan de Oñate had made camp on the bank of the Rio Grande and established the San Gabriel colony. This energetic and accomplished Hispanic woman would develop a passion for the embroidery of her ancestors. She would activate and anchor a lively, loving, long-lived revival of the old Spanish colonial embroidery in northern New Mexico and keep the tradition from disappearing in the twentieth century.

Church at Santa Cruz, New Mexico. *Photo by Jesse Nusbaum, 1911. This image of the old Santa Cruz church was taken a decade before Teofila and Pedro Lujan were married there. Courtesy Photo Archives, Palace of the Governors (MNM/DCA), Santa Fe (negative 061692).*

PART TWO

Revival of Colcha Embroidery: Teofila the Activist

KAADTS

CHAPTER 5

Daughter of the Colonists

Maria Adela Teofila Ortiz Lujan was born November 11, 1895, in the small farming village of El Guique. The village sits on the western bank of the Rio Grande, just two miles north of the site of San Gabriel del Yunque — the first permanent Spanish settlement in New Mexico and first capital of the province. During a life that spanned nearly one hundred years, Teofila would demonstrate the same independence, initiative, and endurance as women in centuries past who managed to scratch out an existence in Spain's isolated and hostile frontier kingdom. By melding the old way of life with good things the new century offered — education and the opportunity to earn a paycheck — this daughter of the colonists was able to instill a love of tradition in her own family and pioneer a revival of the waning practice of colcha embroidery in her community.

Teofila's birth is registered in the same church records as the birth of her mother, her maternal grandfather, and her great-grandfather. This spirited woman who took such pride in her own self-reliance enjoyed telling the story of her maternal grandmother, Maria Gregarita López, who was kidnapped by Indians. Born in 1836 somewhere on the northern frontier of the new republic of Mexico, Gregarita was only seven years old when a party of marauding Comanches captured her and carried her north to their village. Sometime later, a group of *fleteros*, Spanish traders who traveled the plains, passed through the Comanche village. The young girl seized the opportunity. She bolted to the traders and begged them to take her away.

Opposite: Three children of Amado and Refugio Ortiz. Teofila, the oldest daughter, is in the center. Courtesy of Esther Vigil.

Teofila's father and mother, Amado and Refugio Ortiz, married on June 27, 1892, in the church at San Juan Pueblo. Courtesy of Esther Vigil.

Traded for a sack of flour and some bread, the girl, who would be remembered by her descendants as Mama Vita, returned with the fleteros to their home in Villita, New Mexico. There she was adopted and raised by the López family. At age thirteen, she married Juan B. López in the San Juan Church at Ohkay Owingeh Pueblo.

Mama Vita's granddaughter Teofila married into another Hispanic family that had deep roots in the soil of northern New Mexico. Lujans had lived and farmed in the watershed of the upper Rio Grande since shortly after Oñate established the San Gabriel colony in 1598. The birth of one descendant, Francisco de Lujan, was recorded in 1611 in the settlement of Taos, some forty miles up the river from San Gabriel.

Another descendant, Juan Domingo Lujan, was born in 1655 and lived in Santa Fe, which had become the new capital of the province in 1610 after the failure of Oñate's colony. He married Juana de Mendoza. Their son, Juan Lujan, was born in 1678 — less than two years before the Pueblo Revolt. When the Indians of the Rio Grande pueblos united to attack and destroy the Spanish settlements and mission churches, the terrified young couple must have walked the three hundred dusty miles to refuge in El Paso with their two-year-old son and the other survivors.

Six years after Diego de Vargas and his soldiers regained control of the province for Spain and resumed the process of colonization, twenty-year-old Juan Lujan, who as a toddler had fled to safety with his parents, returned to Santa Fe. There he married Maria Martin Serrano, a young woman whose father, D. Martin Serrano, had been born in 1630 in the vicinity of Santa Cruz and had lived there all his life. His was one of the families that had apparently decided to stay and work their land rather than follow Governor Peralta to the new settlement in Santa Fe.

The Lujan–Serrano newlyweds headed to Santa Cruz and continued their parents' efforts to make the colony their home. The birth of their son, Juan José Lujan, was recorded in the San Ildefonso Pueblo church. Construction of a new church for the villa of Santa Cruz was begun in 1733. Thereafter, the marriage of every Lujan in the line of Juan José was listed in the records of the Santa Cruz church. Teofila would marry Pedro Lujan there on December 30, 1920.

As outside interests began to encroach, in 1893 Juan Ponciano Lujan, Teofila's future father-in-law, joined with eighteen other individuals to petition the U.S. government to confirm their ownership of the tracts of land that their ancestors had been granted in the area of Santa Cruz under Spanish law. The Santa Cruz Land Grant petition argued that

> they and their heirs and assigns have continued to occupy, possess and hold the same from the time the same was granted to them to the present time, continuously, openly and notoriously [*sic*] residing upon, cultivating the same as far as the same was susceptible of cultivation, and otherwise using and occupying the same as they had a right to do under the laws and customs which have prevailed in New Mexico since the date of said different decrees or grants, made between 1695 and 1706 by Diego de Vargas and Pedro R. Cubero, each being Governor and Captain General of the Province of New Mexico.

On a June day in 1892, Maria de Refugio López, daughter of Mama Vita — the woman kidnapped by Comanches as a young girl — married Amado Ortiz, Teofila's father. Amado, the second of eight children, was a teacher and sheep inspector for the federal government and commuted by horse and buggy to work at various pueblos.

A strong proponent of education, he instilled in his family a love of learning that inspired the young Teofila and was the catalyst for most of her exceptional accomplishments later in life. The first girl of the family's six children, Teofila was very close to her father. She delighted in eliciting a smile of approval from him when she offered a prompt and enthusiastic answer to the question he posed every evening during dinner: "And what did each of you learn today?"

Teofila was only sixteen when her father died. On his deathbed, Amado extracted a promise from his wife to educate all six of their children, the girls as well as the boys. His request was a tall order at that time, in that educational opportunities for men were rare in northern New Mexico. Such opportunities were even rarer for women, who were expected to stay at home. Wondering how she would ever be able to feed and clothe — let alone educate — all her children, who ranged in age from six to eighteen, the devastated widow and her family moved to Santa Fe. Her extended family and four siblings probably pitched in and helped her physically, emotionally, and financially.

Resilient and determined, Teofila managed to fulfill her father's final request. She graduated at age eighteen from the Academy of Our Lady of Light in Santa Fe, later known as Loretto Academy. After graduating, she landed a job at Bond & Nohl, the only mercantile store in the rapidly growing town of Española. With her income, she helped support her mother and siblings. Her facility in English was no doubt a benefit for her Anglo employers; their customers were all local farmers who spoke only Spanish.

Teofila was the first female clerk at Bond & Nohl, and she took great pride in the fact that she had managed to talk them into hiring her. Like Alvina, the resourceful woman who had talked the men of her village into letting her go on a buffalo hunt in the eighteenth century, the tenacious and self-reliant young graduate exceeded the expectations of her community and her culture.

The store was the center of economic life and trade in northern New Mexico, prospering because it was able to extend credit for one hundred-pound sacks of staples — sugar, flour, and beans — to families who had seasonal incomes from agriculture and the sale of livestock. Teofila began work in the produce section. At first the men balked at transacting business with a woman. But the confident and personable young graduate gradually won them over with her facility in math and her willingness to do the customers an occasional favor by writing a letter in English on their behalf. Next she worked as a clerk in the clothing section, where she may have gained what her family remembers as a fondness for the one or two quality items of apparel that would last forever. Later in life, she delighted in wearing a smart, wide-brimmed hat to church rather than the standard tápalo donned by most other women in the community.

Then she decided to further her education. Like her father before her, she became a teacher. A new facility, the Spanish American Normal School, had opened in 1909 in the northern community of El Rito. Teofila took advantage of the opportunity and headed off to attend an institution whose first graduating class of eighty-seven students included only seven Hispanics. She completed the school's teacher certification program and received her diploma in 1917, at the age of twenty-two.

Wedding portrait of Teofila and Pedro Lujan, married on December 30, 1920, in the Santa Cruz church. Courtesy of Esther Vigil.

Her first teaching job was in the one-room schoolhouse in El Guique. Most of the students were young men from the surrounding farms. Some were older and taller than Teofila. They welcomed the new teacher to class by sticking pins up through the cushion of her chair. Successfully surviving the challenges of her first classroom, Teofila went on to teach in other communities nearby — Tierra Amarilla, Santa Cruz, La Mesilla — and usually returned to Bond & Nohl for summer employment. She was proud of the fact that even after she started teaching, the store always wanted her to come back and work.

In 1920, the year she turned twenty-five, Teofila married Pedro Lujan and went to live with her husband on his thirty-acre farm in the small community of San Pedro, just across the river from Santa Cruz. She continued teaching until her first child was born the following year, then focused her considerable energy on the traditional job of homemaking.

Harvest near Cuyamungué. *Undated photo by T. Harmon Parkhurst. Well into the twentieth century, farm homes in northern New Mexico had few modern conveniences. Courtesy Photo Archives, Palace of the Governors (MNM/DCA), Santa Fe (negative 004218).*

Daily life in the farming communities of northern New Mexico had changed little in three centuries. Most families still spoke only Spanish. The new bride set up housekeeping in a home that had no electricity or indoor plumbing. The adobe farmhouse and outbuildings were of the same construction and design as those of farms in sixteenth-century Spain. Teofila baked her bread in a *horno,* the outdoor oven that the Spanish had adopted from the Moors. One modern convenience she did have was a factory-made iron cookstove, which had replaced the traditional indoor charcoal cooking fire in northern New Mexico homes by 1900.

At a time when the outdoors was men's domain and women stayed indoors, Teofila scoffed at the stereotype and went out to help Pedro raise animals and crops on the land that his ancestors had cultivated. To water their garden, orchard, and alfalfa fields, they maintained several acequias — irrigation ditches in a communal system that the Spanish had introduced to this arid province. They grew many types of plants that early settlers had brought to the province from New Spain: fruit trees, grapes, chilies, tomatoes. Decades later, her granddaughter Stella, who lived in Albuquerque, enjoyed spending time on the farm with Teofila during school breaks. She loved picking berries from the bushes that grew along one of the acequias, climbing trees, and eating delicious fresh meat and vegetables from the farm. Stella vividly recalls the excitement and delight of working with Teofila in the pump house to make jam on the big iron cookstove that had been moved there when the family got an electric stove for the kitchen. The wood fire crackled and glowed in the belly of the old stove as they stirred huge, bubbling pots of sweetened berries and tended a tin can full of melted paraffin to seal the hot jars of jam. The nimble young girl was adept at scrambling up branches in the orchard to tie up tin pie plates, which spun in the breeze to scare birds away from the ripe peaches, apples, pears, apricots, and cherries.

Stella also recalls her grandmother's steadfast dedication to, and love for, her religion. The Catholic faith that the Spanish had brought to the New World was an important source of strength for the colonists of New Mexico, and the faith of her ancestors sustained and brought joy to Teofila during her entire life. Stella remembers what a special occasion her grandma made of the fifth day of each month, when it was her family's turn to host the Sagrada Familia (Holy Family). When the *capillita* (small shrine) arrived, Teofila would place it on her bedroom chest of drawers, open the doors of the portable shrine, and burn candles day and night to honor and venerate the presence of the Holy Family of Nazareth: Jesus, Mary, and Joseph. Specific prayers and devotions were offered to the family during the day it was in residence.

Figures of the saints have been important and beloved members of Catholic households in New Mexico since colonial times and continue in that role today. Father Salvador Gené, a Franciscan from Barcelona, Spain, arrived in 1920 to serve the parish of Santa Cruz. He belonged to the Sons of the Holy Family, a congregation founded by Father José Manyanet in Spain in 1864. Father Gené introduced his practice to the Santa Cruz community. Today about thirty *coros* in the parish honor the Holy Family. Each coro is a society of thirty households with a custodian responsible for the organization of the society. Each coro has its own capillita, which resides one day each month in every household in the coro. On the annual feast day of the Holy Family, members of the various coros gather at the church with their capillitas to attend mass.

There was a small public school in San Pedro, just a mile and a quarter down the hill from the Lujan farm. A few years after the birth of her second child, Teofila decided to start teaching again. She was responsible for pupils in the fifth, sixth, and seventh grades, whom she taught in the larger of the school's two classrooms. Fred Vigil, one of her sixth graders, remembers her as a kind but stern instructor. He says she was a very knowledgeable teacher who was especially sharp in arithmetic. She made sure the students knew their multiplication tables. Fred recalls standing outside the school to see if she was coming, and watching her walk across the fields of neighboring farms. Sometimes when it snowed, the students would say, "She won't be coming," but she never failed them, rain or shine. They knew how badly she wanted everyone to learn, because she understood how important it was to have an education. If students weren't paying attention, she'd admonish them by saying, *"El tiempo perdido los Santos lo Iloran"* (Time lost or wasted, the saints cry).

Fred was a lifelong friend of Teofila's son Eddie, and the two boys were fond of hatching schemes to earn money. In those days, most families were very poor. The boys set traps for skunks and muskrats, which they sold for their skins. When they were getting the animals out of the traps, the bad smell sometimes stuck to their clothes. One day, as Fred stood warming himself by the stove in Teofila's classroom, the other pupils began to wrinkle their noses and giggle. She lost no time in sending Fred and his smelly clothes home from school for the remainder of the day.

Fred and Eddie came up with a surefire plan to earn money by delivering newspapers. Customers paid the delivery boys for their newspapers a month in advance. When it was time to pay the newspaper office at the end of their first month of deliveries, the young entrepreneurs found they were short of cash — they had already spent much of what they had collected. Teofila again had to step in and apply corrective action. She paid the balance of what the boys owed the newspaper — but only once. Fred remembers that she gave them so much hell that they never dared make that mistake again.

As responsibilities mounted and her family increased in size, Teofila often faced the same challenge as northern New Mexico women of centuries past — summoning the strength to carry on during the absence of her husband. Like pioneer women whose men were mustered into the provincial militia and sent off to fight in retaliatory campaigns against marauding Comanches, the daughter of the colonists had to manage the farm, livestock, and children single-handedly while Pedro was away for months at a time. After the fall apple harvest, he would drive his wagon as far as Texas to get a fair price for the fruit. In the winter, Pedro and other men of the community were sometimes gone for several months earning wages in the mines around Leadville, Colorado.

The Lujans raised their own four children, as well as the two children of Teofila's younger sister Ernestine, who died from burns suffered in a stove fire. Over the years, they also took in thirty-two foster children age six and older, who stayed until the state found homes for them — some for days, some for months, and a few for years. The oldest was a Mr. Green, a gentleman who lived with the Lujans until he died at the age of eighty. The industrious Teofila also took advantage of several opportunities for income that were offered by the Works Progress Administration (WPA) in the mid-1930s. She taught mattress making in the large garage that housed many of their farm tools and raised baby chickens in incubators.

Teofila was thirty-eight in 1933, when her last child, Esther, was born. That same year, the busy woman with seemingly boundless initiative made the acquaintance of another high-energy woman who lived just a few miles away and was, like herself, an educator. Her new friend, Regina Cata, introduced her to the traditional colcha embroidery of their ancestors, a relaxing pastime and rewarding activity that Teofila became addicted to and pursued for the rest of her life with increasing passion and dedication.

CHAPTER 6
The Arte Antiguo

New Mexico's second official villa, Santa Cruz de la Cañada, was one of the epicenters of the practice of colcha embroidery. One of the earliest written references to the embroidery is in the records of the Santa Cruz church, where Teofila and Pedro exchanged their wedding vows. An 1818 inventory indicates that women in Chimayó, just eight miles up the road from Santa Cruz, were embroidering items for a shop that generated income to maintain the adjacent chapel.

But the embroidery practice was essentially abandoned by the time Teofila and her mentor Regina Cata became deeply involved with the needlework. The two were kindred spirits, gregarious individuals who enjoyed one another's company and shared a deep pride in their heritage. It was these two friends and a number of other Hispanic women in nearby neighborhoods who formed the Arte Antiguo — the social club that would play a pivotal role in the twentieth-century revival of the ancient art of colcha embroidery. For more than sixty years, members of the club held monthly meetings to share information about patterns and supplies, work on colcha projects, and enjoy one another's company.

Club members encouraged and challenged each other and set out to learn all they could about the subject. They traveled to old churches and chapels in northern New Mexico to examine embroidery on vintage altar cloths. They ferreted out and copied the designs of an-

Opposite: Arte Antiguo members wear family heirlooms and vintage clothing to celebrate the club's twenty-fifth anniversary. Courtesy Esther Vigil.

tique embroideries tucked away in their neighbors' attics and cedar chests. They went down to Santa Fe and sketched the patterns of old colchas in museums and private collections.

The club had started in 1928 as an informal social group of Hispanic women. The group met occasionally to listen to speakers and display their family heirlooms—dresses, shoes, jewelry, needlework. The speaker at their first get-together was Fabiola C. de Baca Gilbert, a state extension service agent and scion of an old Spanish family from Las Vegas, New Mexico. She taught the women how to do leatherwork and make felt hats.

On March 31, 1934, the club emerged as a formal organization with an official name — the Arte Antiguo. Its members had decided to focus exclusively and seriously on colcha embroidery. The charter meeting was held at the home of Rose Baca, credited as founder of the club. Assisting in the planning of that first official meeting were Celestina Espinosa, who gave the club its name, and Regina Cata.

Teofila always maintained that it was Regina Cata who inspired the club to sharpen its focus and develop in-depth expertise in the practice of colcha embroidery. The woman was a natural leader, endowed with the patience and interpersonal skills of an effective teacher. She was strong, self-assured, and energetic and had a winning sense of humor that put others at ease.

Cata was born in 1886 in the San Luis Valley of southern Colorado. Her paternal grandfather was from Spain. Her family was en route to California shortly after the turn of the century when their wagon broke down near Ohkay Owingeh Pueblo. While they were waiting for the vehicle to be repaired, Regina met and fell in love with Eulogio Cata, who taught school in nearby Hernandez and later served as governor of the pueblo. The rest of the family left for California, and the fifteen-year-old bride moved into her husband's ancestral home on the pueblo. There she succeeded in making a productive and fulfilling life for herself.

She is remembered for initiating a number of cultural revival projects. The Museum of New Mexico credits her with leading the 1930 revival of the pottery tradition of Ohkay Owingeh Pueblo. Inspired by the revival work of potters Nampeyo of Hopi and Maria Martínez of nearby San Ildefonso Pueblo, she and several women from her adopted pueblo set out to examine the pottery shards at an abandoned ancestral village across the Rio Grande from present-day Ohkay Owingeh. They selected as their model a traditional polished, incised ware that dated to the late fifteenth century. A gregarious and enthusiastic instructor who was admired for her skills, Cata also launched a revival of the "Indian embroidery stitch," or split stitch. She taught embroidery at the Santa Fe Indian School, where students learned the traditional Pueblo needle art — bold, parallel stitches worked in straight-line, geometric patterns.

There's little doubt that Regina Cata was also responsible for inspiring her Hispanic sisters in the Arte Antiguo to get serious about revitalizing the practice of colcha embroidery. The skillful needle artist must have taught them by example. A dramatic embroidery that hangs in the San Juan church at Ohkay Owingeh Pueblo testifies to her talent. This beautifully executed wool-on-wool colcha is approximately four feet by six feet and depicts the Virgin of Guadalupe. It took Cata ten years to complete.

Libby Cata Marcus, one of Regina's five daughters, explained that her mother promised to complete an embroidery in honor of the Virgin, in the hope that the Virgin would bring all the men from her pueblo home safely from World War II. She began the piece in 1941, stitching it with both store-bought and hand-dyed yarns. Barbara Faucon, a granddaughter who studied and documented the extraordinary embroidery, says that her grandmother dyed the yarn to get the exact colors she wanted. To produce the pale yellow, she used corn pollen; for the dark green, wild spinach.

After Regina Cata sparked the Arte Antiguo colcha initiative in 1934, she moved on to other projects. Then Teofila threw herself into what would become a lifelong campaign to fan the flame of the embroidery tradition and keep the fire burning. Five of the club's charter members disappeared abruptly from the roster in 1935 — as though there had been a purge. Most of the women who remained in the club were in Teofila's direct sphere of influence: Aggie Serna, her closest friend; Syria Lucero, a relative's wife; Josie Delgado, a friend and neighbor in San Pedro. Elected to fill the early vacancies were women with strong connections to colcha embroidery. One of them was Eloisa Maestas, a fellow teacher and neighbor of Teofila's in San Pedro, who joined the Arte Antiguo in 1936. Maestas's great-grandmother had owned a shawl with colcha stitching. Her aunt had done embroidery on sabanilla when Eloisa was a young girl.

The women were now totally focused on their stated objective: to have a social club that would rejuvenate the old embroidery tradition. The Arte Antiguo adopted a set of bylaws and established a checking account. The club collected dues each month and kept attendance records. Minutes were recorded in Spanish. The women voted on expenditures and elected officers to serve for the year. The club met monthly at the home of members, in alphabetical order by last name. There was an established format for the meetings — first a brief business session, then work on their embroidery, then a potluck luncheon.

Membership was limited to twelve, and it was understood that every member took considerable pride in her Hispanic heritage. When a vacancy occurred, the women nominated candidates. The person elected to fill the vacancy had to be approved by a majority of the members. As their first project, new members were required to embroider identical wool-on-cotton bedspreads in designs said to be 150 years old. That initial project could take anywhere from one to four years to complete.

The name Teofila Lujan appears in practically every newspaper article ever published about the club's meetings and activities. She and most of her recruits appear in a photograph taken to illustrate a newspaper story about the celebration of the club's twenty-fifth anniversary in 1959. Teofila and her friends are decked out in vintage dresses and hats. Broad smiles testify to their enduring camaraderie. From a later clipping we learn that four of the club's charter members — Teofila Lujan, Aggie Serna, Josie Delgado, and Rose Baca — were still active participants in 1967. Another clipping from the 1960s indicates that Teofila gave a talk and demonstration of the embroidery to the San Gabriel Historical Society.

Tillie Gonzalez, one of the last living members of the Arte Antiguo, spoke of her participation in the club with love and pride. The petite, genteel lady, who was born in Chimayó and attended school in Santa Cruz, said that being elected a member was one of the most exciting events of her life. She remembers that everyone was eager to show the others what they had done on their embroidery since the last meeting. And they all wanted to learn the technique from Teofila and Aggie — the club's two oldest and most respected members. Teofila always told them that their work should look just as good when turned over as it did right side up.

Gonzalez smiled as she recalled how much fun they had. Although they were totally serious about their mission of reviving colcha embroidery, they also enjoyed a good party. Rodeo, fiesta — they did it all. Club member and seamstress Pita Salazar created the elaborate historical costumes for the annual Oñate Fiesta in Española. Because of its commitment to the area's Hispanic heritage, the club was widely respected in the community. In 1976 the fiesta council asked the Arte Antiguo to serve as grand marshals of the fiesta parade. A newspaper article noted that "The members didn't enjoy the weekend Fiestas as centerpieces entirely. They worked diligently [making food] in preparation for a private party of over 450 guests at Max and Anadelle Sánchez' house." The guest list for that party included New Mexico Governor Jerry Apodaca and United States Senator Joe Montoya. Hostess Anadelle Sánchez was a daughter of Aggie Serna, one of the charter members of the Arte Antiguo.

The women made gifts and celebrated one another's birthday at the monthly meetings. They drew names and exchanged presents at their annual Christmas party. They also held special celebrations during the year. Husbands joined them for the gala New Year's dinner at a local restaurant. Families and friends were invited to their picnic each summer. Gonzalez recalls that the club rented a cabin up in the mountains, where it was cool and shady. Members prepared all the food and went to set up the event the day before. The newspaper reported that eighty-five people attended the picnic held on a Sunday afternoon in 1961 at the Pecos Canyon Lodge: "A field mass was said by Fr. Leo Lucero, and sisters from the Pecos Church played guitar. Fry fish was served." Father Lucero was a son of Syria Lucero, one of Teofila's recruits in 1935.

One summer the Arte Antiguo hosted an engagement party for another son of the then-deceased Syria Lucero, and his fiancée. The women served dips, chicken sandwiches, and homemade cakes to one hundred and fifty guests at a member's home, which they had decorated with flowers from another member's garden. According to a newspaper clipping, "Music from the hi-fi was piped onto the patio by speaker for dancing, and the couple opened their many gifts."

Stella Marquez, the granddaughter who spent so many summers in San Pedro with Teofila, remembers attending Arte Antiguo meetings. She was the only young person there and tried to make herself useful. She helped the women trace patterns, listened to their friendly banter as they worked on their stitching, fetched glasses of water, and tidied up after the luncheon. As they worked, the women discussed designs, complained about the quality of a fabric, and shared where they had bought some nice cotton yardage or a hard-to-find color of yarn — generally at stores in Santa Fe. The young girl was struck by how particular the women were about their work. The yarn and fabric had to be just right to achieve the effect they wanted. She also was impressed that they were all such close friends and took such good care of one other. They celebrated their accomplishments, shared updates about their families, and cooked meals to help members who were sick.

When Stella was old enough to drive, she chauffeured her grandmother to meetings. She recalls thinking it was ironic that even though the members of the Arte Antiguo were passionately concerned about keeping the embroidery tradition alive, they remained highly selective about who joined their club. They spent a great deal of time discussing the qualifications of potential members.

They were also selective about whom they taught. Stella remembers hearing one member request permission from the others to teach someone outside the club. She says the women considered themselves guardians of a sacred tradition. They seemed to believe that colcha embroidery was not something that just anyone could sit down and do properly.

Other Revival Efforts in New Mexico

Other groups complemented and amplified the work of the Arte Antiguo to save the needlework of Spanish colonial New Mexico. Their efforts were spawned in a wave of revival movements that flowed from the arts and crafts movement in England and swept the United States and other parts of the world during the early years of the twentieth century (Nunn 2001:28). The revivalists launched a massive effort to document, preserve, and foster the practice of folk arts of cultures they feared were in danger of disappearing.

Artists, health seekers, writers, and philanthropists who migrated to New Mexico soon after it achieved statehood in 1912 became infatuated with the state's exotic Native American and Hispanic cultures. Various newcomers began to collect and document rapidly disappearing examples of Spanish folk art. They developed plans to revive traditional weaving, tinwork, woodcarving, furniture making, and embroidery. They also established standards for what they defined as authentic Spanish folk art.

The Spanish Colonial Arts Society was founded in 1925 by two Santa Fe residents who hoped to stem the tide of loss of traditional Hispanic arts and crafts. Mary Austin, a writer, and Frank Applegate, an artist and collector who lived across the street from Austin, recruited members to work in their fledgling organization. By 1929 the newly incorporated Spanish Colonial Arts Society was actively soliciting donations and purchasing items for its collection.

One of its first acquisitions was the historic Santuario de Chimayó. With funds from an anonymous donor, the society purchased the building and gave it to the Archdiocese of Santa Fe. When Applegate died in 1931, the society purchased many items from his personal collection of Spanish colonial arts, which included colcha embroideries. Ten of those colchas were loaned to the Museum of New Mexico for display in the Palace of the Governors in 1934 — the year the Arte Antiguo held its first official meeting.

From 1926 to 1934, the Spanish Colonial Arts Society held a yearly exhibit and sale of traditional Spanish crafts in the patio of the Museum of Fine Arts in conjunction with the Santa Fe Fiesta. (The fiesta is a September event that celebrates Spain's reconquest of the capital city in 1692 and reestablishment of its colony after the Pueblo Revolt.) Exhibitors had the unprecedented opportunity to compete for cash awards from the society and sell their work to visitors. Today the society continues that tradition. It conducts Spanish Market, a major tourism event, on the Santa Fe Plaza in July and a smaller-scale market indoors in December.

The society experienced a lull in activity after Mary Austin's death in 1934 but was reactivated in 1951 thanks to a community effort led by artist and historian E. Boyd. Boyd published her seminal work *Popular Arts of Spanish New Mexico* in 1974 and served as curator of the society's collection until her death. That collection continues to expand and is housed today in the Museum of Spanish Colonial Art, which opened in 2002 in Santa Fe.

As a distinctive New Mexico art form, colcha embroidery received considerable attention, as well as national exposure, in New Deal-era art programs. In her book *Sin Nombre,* Tey Marianna Nunn describes various embroidery projects done in federally funded art programs across the state during the 1930s. Girls at the National Youth Administration (NYA) camp in Capitan, New Mexico, produced an illustrated catalog from which customers could order items of clothing decorated with colcha embroidery: blouses, aprons, handkerchiefs, jacket vests. Young women from the NYA program in Roswell designed a stage curtain for the Roswell Federal Art Center and embellished it with colcha embroidery. Anglo and Hispanic women in Estella Garcia's WPA colcha class in Melrose, New

"Colcha no. 2" in the 1935 instruction booklet, the wool-on-cotton tablecloth measuring 43 by 52 inches. Photo by Lila L. Scott. Courtesy Curtin-Paloheimo Collection, Acequia Madre House, Santa Fe.

Mexico, collaborated to design and produce embroidered theater curtains, wall hangings, and seat coverings that were used in facilities across the state.

Nunn points out that a photograph of the Roswell NYA class working on their stage curtain appeared in a 1938 issue of *Time* magazine and that other examples of colcha embroidery were exhibited in museums and federal art centers across the country during the New Deal era. One frequently displayed example was included in a WPA exhibit at Bloomingdale's department store in New York City during the 1939 New York World's Fair (Nunn 2001:111).

New Mexico was the first state to obtain federal funds for craft education during the Depression years (Nestor 1978:12). Brice H. Sewell, state director for vocational education and training, was able to hire a small staff to develop a training program through which students could make and sell items to support themselves financially. His staff produced a series of mimeographed booklets that served as the basis of instruction. Each booklet documented a specific craft, providing the history of that particular craft, detailed instructions, and information on traditional materials and designs.

Sewell's staff members Carmen Espinosa, a Spanish teacher and historian, and Dolores Perrault, a weaver and teacher, produced *New Mexico Colonial Embroidery*. The booklet, issued in 1935, featured an introduction written by Espinosa and forty-one pages of colcha designs sketched by Perrault. The source of these designs were historic embroideries owned by Espinosa and by Leonora Curtin, a staunch advocate of the folk arts of Spanish colonial

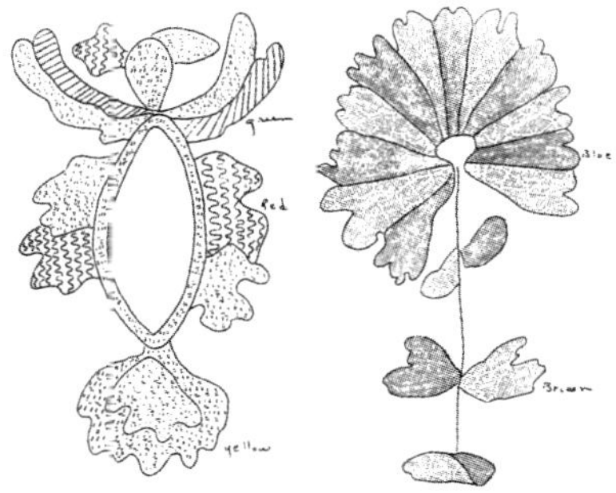

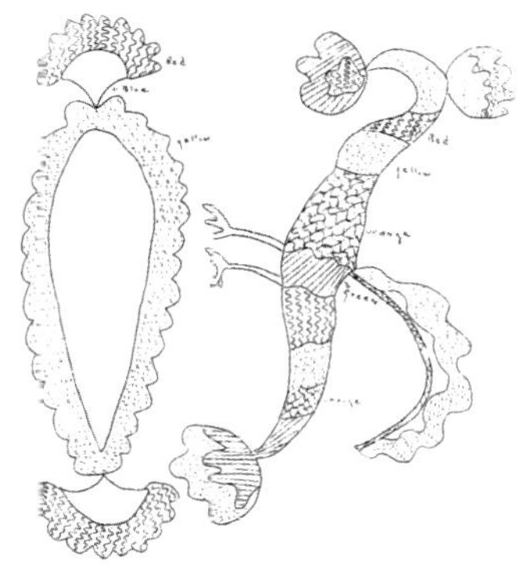

Three pages of motifs from a 1935 New Mexico Department of Vocational Education and Training instruction booklet on colcha embroidery.

The embroidered textile covering the side table appears to be "colcha no. 2" in the 1935 instruction booklet. Courtesy Curtin-Paloheimo Collection, Acequia Madre House, Santa Fe.

New Mexico and an early member of the Spanish Colonial Arts Society.

A passion for folk art ran in Curtin's family. Her maternal grandmother, Eva Scott Fenyes, was an artist of independent means who spent time in New Mexico in the late 1800s and acquired several colcha embroideries. A wool-on-cotton colcha on a side table in a snapshot taken in 1891 in the Fenyes house in Prescott, Arizona, probably is "colcha no. 2" in the New Mexico Department of Vocational Education and Training instruction booklet. This colcha is still part of the Curtin Collection. Eleven different motifs in this particular textile were offered as full-page patterns in the booklet.

Booklet author Carmen Espinosa was a relative of Celestina Espinosa, one of the charter members of the Arte Antiguo, so there is little doubt that members of the club had ready access to the mimeographed instruction booklet. A dresser scarf embroidered by club member Rosa Rodriguez includes the bird motif from "colcha no. 4" in the booklet. Designs from the booklet also appear on bedspreads displayed in a 1954 photo of eight members of the Arte Antiguo.

There were several efforts to provide a sales outlet for revival crafts in New Mexico during the Depression years. But despite attempts to promote the work, colcha embroidery did not sell well. As William Wroth later noted, Hispanic crafts never "caught on" nationally the way Indian crafts did, despite the efforts and enthusiasm of wealthy Anglo patrons (Wroth 1977:6).

In 1930 the Spanish Colonial Arts Society opened The Spanish Arts Shop in Santa Fe. The store was to provide a year-round outlet for revival handiwork. Its letterhead featured an image of colcha embroidery. In what would prove to be an unsuccessful attempt to pro-

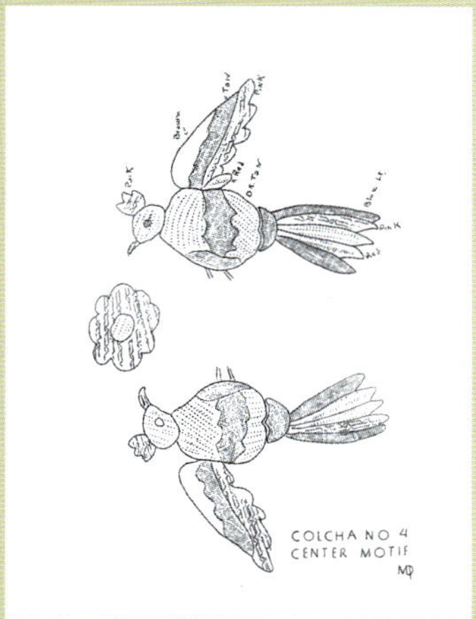

Bird motif from "colcha no. 4" in the 1935 New Mexico Department of Vocational Education and Training instruction booklet.

The bird motif from "colcha no. 4" appears on the dresser scarf embroidered by Rosa Rodriguez, a member of the Arte Antiguo. Photo by Nancy C. Benson. Courtesy of Aurelia Madrid, daughter of Rosa Rodriguez.

Arte Antiguo members display their colcha projects in this 1954 photo. Teofila is second from left; third from left is Rosa Rodriguez. Courtesy of Esther Vigil.

mote the work at the national level, the store dispatched several colchas and other items in its inventory to the American Folk Art Exhibit in Chicago in 1932. Sales were dismal, and the store closed in 1933.

The last manager of the failed venture was Nellie Dunton, an avid embroiderer. Dunton compiled a portfolio of forty plates of motifs she had found on colchas in stores and private collections in Santa Fe. To these illustrations, she added her own observations about the colcha embroidery tradition. A Philadelphia press published her book, *The Spanish Colonial Ornament,* in 1935 (below left).

Undeterred by the failure of The Spanish Arts shop, Leonora Curtin opened her own store to encourage and popularize the Hispanic arts and crafts of New Mexico. The Native Market was a not-for-profit operation subsidized solely by Curtin. It opened in the summer of 1934 on Palace Avenue in Santa Fe and was mentioned in a *Vogue* magazine article two years later (Nestor 1978:32)

The store, which advertised "colcha designs adapted to serve modern needs," sold upholstery and drapery fabric, bedspreads, pillows, cocktail napkins, and tablecloths decorated with the embroidery. For as little as $2.75, customers could purchase wool-on-wool and wool-on-cotton examples that included motifs ranging from geometric designs, zigzag bands

Misconceptions about the History of the Embroidery

Dunton's discussion of the colcha tradition, although thoughtful and comprehensive for its time, contained several naive assertions that were perpetuated in subsequent writings. Her first misconception was that the colcha stitch was the invention of some skilled embroiderer in America. She asserted that the stitch was never used or found on embroideries in Spain or Mexico. This was a major error. In reality, the couching (colcha) stitch was widely used for many centuries by domestic and professional embroiderers in the Old World and was brought to New Spain in the early 1500s. Centuries-old paintings done in both Spain and Mexico portray the couching stitch, and museum collections of historic textiles from Spain and Mexico include the stitch.

Dunton conceded that she did find the colcha stitch on one textile embroidered in Spain in the early seventeenth century, but she concluded that a colonist who had returned from New Mexico had introduced the stitch to Spain. Mary Cabot Wheelwright — a collector and trustee of the Spanish Colonial Arts Society — had it right. In an article published in 1932, she wrote that New Mexico colcha work and designs must have been derived from Mexico (Wheelwright 1932:19).

Opposite: Plate 3 (left) and Plate 12 from The Spanish Colonial Ornament *by Nellie Dunton. Courtesy Museum of Spanish Colonial Art, Collections of the Spanish Colonial Arts Society, Inc., Santa Fe.*

Twin beds and wool-on-cotton colcha bedspreads from the Native Market store in Santa Fe. Photo by Lila L. Scott. Courtesy Curtin-Paloheimo Collection, Acequia Madre House, Santa Fe.

of color, flowers, and leaves to animals such as lions, deer, and birds (Nestor 1978:26)

The Native Market closed in 1940. One of its enduring legacies was the expertise of colcha teacher Tillie Gabaldon Stark, who learned how to do the embroidery while working as an employee of the store. Stark was responsible for preparing the yarn for weaving and needlework. Using a large cauldron at the back of the store, she demonstrated to customers how wool was dyed.

In the course of a long and productive life, Stark won numerous awards at Spanish Market for her embroidery, conducted colcha workshops, and in 1968 went to Washington, D.C., to demonstrate the traditional embroidery of Spanish colonial New Mexico at the Smithsonian Institution's annual American Folklife Festival.

Mormon homesteaders in a small settlement south of Taos, New Mexico, developed the only financially successful colcha sales operation during the Depression years. As the small settlement of Carson struggled in the grip of a drought, the son of its founder took up blanket trading as a source of income. He

Pillows from the Native Market. The pillow covers are solidly embroidered with colcha stitches. Photo by Lila L. Scott. Courtesy Curtin-Paloheimo Collection, Acequia Madre House, Santa Fe.

had an old wool-on-wool colcha that needed to be repaired before he could sell it. By examining the textile, his sister-in-law Frances Graves taught herself how to do the stitch. She began creating wool-on-wool colcha embroideries of her own design. The Graves family sold the first Carson colcha in 1930. Other men and women in the community followed suit, and a successful cottage industry arose.

Most of the Carson colchas were made from worn, ragged textiles that were beyond repair. The workers used old woolen mattress covers as the ground fabric. For embroidery yarn they unraveled sabanilla, as well as Rio Grande, Navajo, and Hopi blankets. Unlike the designs of the historic Spanish colchas, which are floral, flowing, and curvilinear, the images on the Carson colchas tend to be stilted and square. In many examples, the embroidery stitches all run in the same direction rather than following the curves of the design.

Catholic saints, candelabras, horses, Indians, covered wagons, and religious proces-

Top: The needlework signature of Tillie Stark. Photo by Lila L. Scott. Courtesy Curtin-Paloheimo Collection, Acequia Madre House, Santa Fe.

Details of colcha motifs on a wool-on-cotton bedspread measuring 124 by 128 inches. Tillie Stark embroidered the bedspread for Leonora Curtin. Photo by Lila L. Scott. Courtesy Curtin-Paloheimo Collection, Acequia Madre House, Santa Fe.

Top: A Carson colcha done on badly worn sabanilla that was patched with smaller pieces of sabanilla before the embroidery was applied. Photo by Dan Richey. Courtesy of Sharon and Charles Aberle.

Middle: Detail of a Carson colcha showing two characteristic motifs—a Catholic saint (Our Lady of Guadalupe) and a candelabra. Photo by Dan Richey. Courtesy of Sharon and Charles Aberle.

Bottom: Detail of a Carson colcha embroidered with undyed yarn. The image shows a religious procession of the Catholic brotherhood of Penitentes. Photo by Nancy C. Benson.

sions of the Catholic brotherhood of Penitentes were depicted in the colchas made by the Mormon community. Selling for less than half the cost of historic Spanish colchas, the fanciful handiwork made from recycled materials found a ready market in buyers who didn't necessarily realize that the wool-on-wool embroideries were not authentic early pieces.

Of all the colcha revival efforts that sprang up during the 1920s and 1930s in New Mexico, the Arte Antiguo held a unique place. The club was strictly a social organization with no institutional, political, or religious ties. It was the only indigenous group of Hispanic women who produced the traditional embroidery. They did so for more than six decades in the course of more than seven hundred monthly work sessions.

Ethnographer Suzanne MacAulay points out other important distinctions. Because the Arte Antiguo was internally motivated and self-directed, members were free to reinterpret the historic colcha designs according to their own tastes. And unlike participants in federally and state-funded needlework revival groups, they did not sell their embroidery out of economic necessity (MacAulay 2000:82). Club members kept much of their needlework in the hope that the embroidery of their ancestors would help future generations remember and appreciate their Hispanic heritage.

Opposite: A Carson colcha embroidered in natural wool. Museum of Spanish Colonial Art, Collections of the Spanish Colonial, Arts Society, Inc., Santa Fe (1972.6).

CHAPTER 7
Strengthening the Thread

In the early 1940s, the United States shifted its focus and resources to the war effort. As federal funds were diverted to military and defense programs, the wave of revival projects that had swept the country ebbed. In Santa Fe, the Native Market store had closed its doors, and the Spanish Colonial Arts Society was dormant. But it was business as usual for the Arte Antiguo. Teofila and her friends in the Española Valley continued to meet once a month to work on their colcha embroidery and plan new projects.

Teofila was one of the club's most prolific embroiderers, according to her friend Aggie Serna. She remembers that Teofila was consumed by her passion for the embroidery and always took a project with her to work on before meetings started (Morgan 1987). Former student Fred Vigil holds the same memory: She worked hard all day long. But if she ever sat down, there was a needle in her hand.

The homemaker, farmwife, and mother of four still taught school and worked at the Bond & Nohl store. In 1945 she took advantage of a new opportunity. The Atomic Energy Commission was paying good wages for work in Los Alamos. The town on "the Hill," where scientists from many nations had worked in secrecy on the Manhattan Project to develop the atomic bomb, was only seventeen miles from Española.

Teofila applied for a position and was hired as housekeeper of Fuller Lodge, the town's principal building and the social center of wartime Los Alamos. In the course of her years

Opposite: Wool-on-cotton colcha by Teofila Lujan. Photo by Daniel A. Vigil. Courtesy of Esther Vigil.

Clockwise from top left:

Teofila in her mid-fifties. Courtesy of Esther Vigil.

Wool-on-cotton colcha by Teofila Lujan, 21 by 39.5 inches, 1978. Photo by Dan Richey. Courtesy of Nancy C. Benson.

This floral motif from "colcha no. 3" in the instruction booklet often appears in embroidery done by members of the Arte Antiguo.

Detail of the upper-right corner of a colcha embroidered by Teofila, showing a stylized flower motif based on Curtin Collection "colcha no. 3" in the 1935 New Mexico Department of Vocational Education and Training instruction booklet. Photo by Dan Richey.

at the lodge, she got to know many of the now legendary scientists of the Manhattan Project on a first-name basis: Robert Oppenheimer, Edward Teller, Stanislaw Ulam. She and her daughter Esther babysat the Teller and Ulam children.

Teofila was also in charge of recruiting men and women for domestic work in the government dorms that housed the scientific personnel on the Hill. Aggie Serna, her close friend and fellow member of the Arte Antiguo, followed her lead. Their workdays and commute were long. Family needs continued to press. But the women always made time to attend monthly club meetings.

Stella recalls the terror of rushing to a meeting with her high-energy grandma. Generating a cloud of dust behind them, they barreled down the center of San Pedro Road in a little blue Chevy. A car came straight at them, and the young passenger — certain she was about to be killed in the collision — put her hands over her eyes. The oncoming car swerved out of the way, but grandma stayed her course. Teofila continued her trip through life at high speed. During her middle and later years, the energetic and productive woman accelerated her efforts to strengthen the embroidery tradition of her ancestors.

Above: Teofila at age eighty-five. Photo by Nancy C. Benson.

Right: Detail of the flowing, arabesque designs that Teofila loved to use in her needlework. Photo by Nancy C. Benson.

Her cherished friends in the Arte Antiguo were no doubt a source of comfort for her when Pedro died in 1956. In a newspaper photo that same year, we see Teofila and other members exchanging Christmas presents at a club meeting. She is also listed as an attendee in an article about the club's October meeting, which featured a large jack-o'-lantern centerpiece for the refreshment table and sandwiches, salad, cookies, pumpkin pie, and coffee, "in keeping with the Halloween theme."

Widowed at sixty-one, Teofila continued to drive to work on the Hill until she turned seventy. She retired from Los Alamos in 1965 — the same year that E. Boyd, curator of the Spanish Colonial Arts Society's collection, reactivated the society's annual Spanish Market. Decelerating long enough to enjoy a short trip to Mexico to celebrate her retirement, Teofila then sprang back to work full-time as a volunteer instructor of colcha embroidery, quilting, and crocheting at senior citizen centers in Española and Santa Fe. With only herself to care for in the old farmhouse in San Pedro, she had more time to indulge her passion for the embroidery.

In 1966 she began to exhibit her work. That August the Museum of International Folk Art in Santa Fe opened a juried show, the New Mexico Craftsmen's Exhibition, which included one of her embroideries on sabanilla. Her colcha work was displayed with other artistic textiles — yardage of mohair and silk, a wall hanging of hand-spun wool and willow, a mobile of cotton, rayon, and jute. The museum show also included elegant carved doors, a silver perfume vial, a stoneware storage jar with a walnut lid, and a bracelet of walrus ivory with caribou hoof inlay.

That same summer, a colcha bedspread that Teofila and three other members of the Arte Antiguo entered in Spanish Market won an award. In 1968 the Museum of New Mexico purchased a pillow that Teofila had exhibited at Spanish Market. The pillow was covered with pink and white zigzags — the same design that appeared on one of the earliest wool-on-wool colchas. It sold for $7.50.

She continued to exhibit at Spanish Market and garner awards for more than a decade, earning increasing respect for the embroidery. In 1972 the Spanish Colonial Arts Society bought her second-prize colcha sampler. In 1973 there were twenty-two exhibitors at Spanish Market, five in the category of colcha embroidery. Teofila's entry "representing a group of eight women of the Valley" took first prize in the category.

There is no record of her participating again in Spanish Market until 1977, the year she won first prize for an embroidered bedspread and was interviewed by the Museum of International Folk Art for background information for its comprehensive exhibition and publication *Spanish Textile Tradition of New Mexico and Colorado*.

In 1979 she again took first prize at Spanish Market, this time for an embroidered chest cover. The Albuquerque Museum opened its new facility that year with an exhibition called One Culture: Three Visions. The show featured a large wool-on-cotton colcha that Teofila had embroidered.

Teofila in the backyard of her farmhouse in San Pedro, 1980. Photo by Nancy C. Benson.

In 1980, the year she turned eighty-five, the irrepressible advocate of the embroidery received what was probably her most cherished honor — the grand prize (Best of Show) award at Spanish Market. A Santa Fe collector paid $500 for her prize-winning bedspread. By that time, eight U.S. museums had exhibited her work; three held examples of her embroidery in their permanent collections. In early June, the Denver Post's *Empire Magazine* ran a full-color feature story on how she "breathes fresh life into a rapidly disappearing craft" (Benson 1980:50).

Although she had been spending winters in Albuquerque with her daughter Esther since 1970, the woman who took such pride in her independence insisted on spending the balance of the year in her own house in San Pedro. Esther's son Victor remembers that when the family drove up to visit, his grandmother was generally out and about doing her chores when they arrived. It wasn't uncommon to see her hauling two five-gallon buckets half full of feed for the animals, or water for her small patch of flowers.

Her eyesight began to fail when she was eighty-six, so she went to live year-round with Esther's family. Still devoted to her old friends in the Arte Antiguo, Teofila occasionally asked the family to drive her up to a meeting. They also helped her host several meetings at their home in Albuquerque—a strenuous outing for the carpool of aging embroiderers from the Española Valley. By the time she turned eighty-seven, her days of needlework were over. She had lost most of her eyesight to a detached retina and cataracts. Consoled, tended, and treasured by her loving family for the remainder of her years, Teofila died in 1995, just four months before she would have celebrated her one hundredth birthday.

Her funeral mass was celebrated in the venerable old Santa Cruz church. The altar platform was lined with ten Sagrada Familias from the parish, including the one her family had received into their home every month and honored with a candle and special prayers. Grandson Victor read the family's eloquent and fitting eulogy:

> She rushed through this world with grace and with confidence. . . . We learned many things from you, grandmother, and you gave us many values to teach to our own families. Yours is the passing of an era, and the beginning of a legacy. When I think of my grandmother I think of:
>
> The importance of a good education,
> The value of a hard day's work,
> The power of faith,
> The beauty of art.

Her legacy includes activities and accomplishments that helped strengthen the colcha embroidery tradition. The Spanish colonial embroidery that Teofila and the Arte Antiguo took such pleasure in reviving, executing, and exhibiting became a benchmark and inspiration for the next generation of artists who took up the embroidery. One of the leading artists of that generation is her daughter Esther.

Opposite: Altar cloth by Esther Lujan, 1983, made for the main altar of the Santa Cruz church in conjunction with a major restoration of the altar screen and arch. Photo by Tom Velarde.

Wool-on-cotton colcha by Esther Vigil, solid embroidery, 21 by 28 inches framed (see page 154). Photo by Tony Reynolds. Courtesy of Esther Vigil.

PART THREE

Renaissance of Colcha Embroidery: Esther the Artist

CHAPTER 8

Child in a World Unchanged by Time

Esther Grace Lujan, the fourth child of Teofila and Pedro, was born in the spring of 1933 during a three-year drought that took a serious toll on crops in northern New Mexico. The obstacles the farmers in the upper Rio Grande Valley faced that year were the same ones the Spanish colonists had encountered when they first began working the fields in that arid land. Prolonged droughts, hailstorms, and insects destroyed their crops periodically. A hard freeze in late spring killed the blossoms and buds on their fruit trees. Disease decimated their livestock. But the young Esther was only vaguely aware of how the grown-ups struggled to feed and raise their families in that isolated rural enclave that had changed so little over the centuries.

She has vivid memories of growing up in San Pedro. Their adobe farmhouse had no gas or electricity, no running water. Everyone knew everyone else in the tightly knit farming community. Its residents were bound together by their reverence for the Catholic faith and the traditions of their ancestors who had settled the valley centuries earlier.

English was a foreign language. It was spoken by only a small fraction of the people in the community. Both Spanish and English were spoken in the Lujan home. Although he understood English, Pedro spoke only Spanish and expected the children to reply in Spanish. Teofila communicated with her family in English because she understood the importance of being bilingual in a changing world.

Opposite: Detail of the central motif in one of Esther's colchas (see page 157), showing the finely executed stitches. Photo by Tony Reynolds.

A wood-burning stove warmed Esther's bedroom, but the fire never lasted through the night. She believes that the earliest colonists began doing colcha embroidery for a highly practical reason — they needed the warmth to survive. She has a great deal of empathy for her ancestors when she recalls how hard it was to get up, especially during the winter, when the room was freezing cold and it felt so good to be under the covers. The old colchas were indeed warm. They were essentially three layers of wool — the sabanilla, plus the solid stitching on top and lots of yarn on the reverse side. In an unpublished manuscript written in the 1930s, Mary Austin, one of the founders of the Spanish Colonial Arts Society, made a similar observation about a wool-on-wool colcha. She noted that its weight was such that it made a very warm as well as beautiful bedcover (Applegate and Austin n.d.:115 – 16).

Most of the food on the family's table came from the vegetable garden, animal pens, and orchards that Esther could survey from her bedroom window. She still treasures the memory of how good that food tasted. Crunchy, tart green apples picked before they ripened and doused with salt. Tender stalks of wild asparagus dug with a knife as the tips just peeked above ground. Succulent pork roasted all night in a covered pit and served to guests celebrating a baptism, confirmation, or wedding. No apricots were ever as large and sweet as the ones that grew on the tree near the banks of the irrigation ditch.

Milk was rich and thick with cream, which was churned into fresh butter. For breakfast, Teofila sometimes served cinnamon-laced *natillas,* a puddinglike dessert made with milk, egg yolks, and egg whites that were whipped and folded into the mixture. With the surplus milk, she made *requeson* (cheese) that Pedro sliced and slathered with homemade jelly.

Neighbors took food to the sick and tended the elderly. Most of the older women wore long black skirts and blouses and covered their head with tápalos, black shawls that obscured part of their faces. It was customary for widows to wear black during a period of mourning, which generally lasted two years. But there was no way to tell which of those somber figures really was a widow and which was simply wearing the color as practical, everyday attire.

Children were to be seen but not heard and to respect their elders. Women and girls always wore head coverings in church, and men removed their hats. From the young girl's perspective, her world was populated by a confusing continuum of grown-ups. In addition to the numerous relatives by blood, there were all of her parents' *comadres* and *compadres* — relatives by baptism, confirmation, or marriage. The appropriate greeting to all was a ceremonious *"buenos dias le de Dios"* (God grant you a good day).

Hospitality was a virtue in the community. The coffeepot on the back burner of a family's woodstove was put to heat the minute a visitor came through the door. One memorable visitor was Don Eppifanio, the *mayordomo* of the acequias. His job was to apportion the water and patrol the ditches at night to see that no one irrigated without permission.

The short, jovial gentleman sometimes stopped by the Lujan home in the evenings and chatted with the family over a hot cup of coffee. He was an inveterate storyteller, and the children sat entranced as he spun his tales of *brujas* (witches) and El Coco (the boogeyman). The most frightening figure of all was La Llorona, the infamous wailing woman. She murdered her own child and is said to wander the fields and ditch banks after midnight, shrieking and moaning in remorse over her terrible deed.

After Don Eppifanio finished his stories, the children were sent to bed. Esther said her prayers, but it was hard to fall asleep in the darkness. Hearing the mournful wail of a coyote, she shivered in fear as she conjured up an image of the dreaded La Llorona walking out by the irrigation ditch.

Water is the lifeblood of lands with little rain. Settlers from arid regions in southern Spain had brought to New Mexico the knowledge of a system to govern the building, maintenance, and distribution of water for irrigation. The Lujan family got water for their animals, alfalfa field, garden, and orchard from two community acequias. When little or no water flowed in the ditches, Pedro loaded large metal barrels on the horse-drawn farm wagon and herded the cows and horses to the river, where they drank while he filled the barrels with water for the rest of the animals.

To hedge against dry periods, he dug and cemented the walls of a deep reservoir near the upper ditch. When there was ample rainfall, water from the ditch overflowed into the reservoir. Esther muses that although they didn't have any money for luxuries, they did have their very own swimming pool right there in the front yard. It didn't do them any good, though, because none of them knew how to swim.

But they certainly knew how to enjoy themselves with everyone else in the community. Saint's day celebrations were a popular religious devotion in medieval Europe, and Juan de

Oñate enacted the first one in New Mexico on June 24, 1598, when he stopped en route to founding Spain's first colony to honor his namesake, Saint John (Juan). The twenty-ninth of June on the Catholic calendar is Saint Peter's (Pedro's) Day, and the community of San Pedro always held a celebration in his honor. First thing in the morning, the parish priest from the Santa Cruz church came to conduct mass in the tiny chapel in San Pedro, where everyone had gathered. After the blessing, they went home to celebrate, socialize, and receive visitors.

For the Lujan open house on San Pedro Day, Teofila prepared *biscochitos* (sugar cookies) and *empanaditas* (little pies). She offered guests glasses of her famous red wine — a sweet beverage made from chokecherries that grew on bushes between the upper and lower irrigation ditch. Pedro made root beer, beer, and soda pop for the open house and other celebrations. He poured the beverages into individual glass bottles, capped the bottles, and put them up in the attic to ferment. Every so often, Esther heard a sharp ping in the dark; one of the bottles had popped its top.

Early in the harvest season, when the green chili was mature, women harvested the first part of the chili crop. They roasted, peeled, and canned the green chili for use over the winter, or hung it in the sun to dry. They left the balance of the crop on the vine until the chilies turned bright red. Then neighbors gathered in each other's *despensas* (barns where hay was stored) to help tie the red chilies into *ristras*.

Participants formed an assembly line to make the ristras. Some sorted the chilies. The next group tied three or four chilies by their stems to a short length of cotton twine at intervals of four to six inches. Others completed the job by braiding the clusters on the twine onto a long strand of jute that hung from the wall.

As the neighbors worked, they swapped stories, laughed, and perhaps hummed along as an elder played the old songs on a fiddle. They tied together the two ends of each strand of jute and hung the oblong wreathes outside on a south-facing wall to dry in the sun. Women used the dried chilies from their ristras — a staple in every kitchen — to cook batches of *chile caribe,* a zesty sauce made with pork that was spooned over everything from pinto beans and eggs to patties of mashed potatoes.

On the fifth day of every month, it was her family's turn to receive their society's Sagrada Familia into their home. Esther has vivid memories of feeling excited and close to her family on the days they joined together to express their devotion to the Holy Family.

When the traveling shrine arrived, the Lujans lit a candle that was left to burn the whole time the Holy Family was in residence. In the evening, they knelt together to pray aloud to the carved relief figures of Jesus, Mary, and Joseph, encased in the wooden shrine behind glass. Teofila led the prayers.

Every Saturday night there were standard preparations for attending church the next morning. Water for bathing was toted up to the house from the well by the lower irrigation ditch and heated on the woodstove. Scrubbed and shampooed, Esther spent an uncomfortable night sleeping with her long wet hair wrapped around homemade curlers to make her look her "Shirley Temple" best.

The whole family headed off to church early on Sunday, fasting before taking communion. They sat in the same pew every week, five or six rows from the front and directly under the pulpit from which Father Salvador delivered the sermon. Sitting quietly and paying attention for what seemed like an interminable period of time was a challenge for the active young girl. Mass was still said in Latin, a language that was incomprehensible to most attendees. The service lasted for an hour or more. Father Salvador loomed above her, almost within arms' reach.

Sunday was a day of rest for everyone in the family except her mother. Teofila still had to spend the day cooking because there were always neighbors and family dropping in for a visit after church. On the way home from church, the Lujans stopped by the garden — a large field surrounded by a barbed-wire fence to keep out the animals. Someone would step on the lower wire of the fence and stretch open the upper wire so the others could gain access. Teofila gathered up her skirt and climbed through the fence to pick fresh produce for the big midday meal — corn, green chili, cantaloupe, watermelons.

Esther relishes the memory of herself as a tomboy who loved to tag along with her father and help outdoors with the chores — pitching hay, hoeing, irrigating, picking fruit, or just heading down the hill with her salt shaker to munch on those green apples, radishes, tomatoes, and cucumbers. When she wasn't roaming outside, she did her best to help with the household chores so that Teofila didn't have as much to do when she came home from work. One day after school, Esther decided to surprise her mother by doing some canning. She prepared the fruit to be canned but lost her courage to complete the project when she thought about using the big pressure cooker. She was scared it would explode.

In her early years of grade school, she became obsessed with owning her own bicycle. Teofila agreed to pay half the cost of a bike if Esther could earn the other half, and her dad offered her an opportunity to earn money. He paid a nickel for every bushel of apples she harvested. She strapped on the twill harness, which supported a canvas bag that was almost as big as she was. Then she climbed a tree in the orchard and loaded her bag so full that Pedro sometimes had to help her get back down. But the nickels she earned didn't turn into dollars quickly enough.

It seemed as though it would take forever to save enough money, so she found an additional source of income: a newspaper delivery route. Putting a bridle on the family horse, La Blue—whom she was accustomed to riding without a saddle — the papergirl mounted and headed off to begin her weekend deliveries. The first outing went smoothly — until the old horse caught sight of the dirt road to his barn and broke into a gallop. Caught off guard, Esther lost her grip on the reins and fell to the ground frighteningly close to a barbed-wire fence. Dusting herself off, she headed home on foot and prayed that nobody had seen her embarrassing landing.

The next time she made her deliveries, the tenacious girl was ready for the home stretch. She flattened herself against the horse's neck and held on for dear life as La Blue shot up the hill, clattered across the second bridge over the irrigation ditch, and came to an abrupt halt in front of his corral.

With dogged determination, she finally managed to get enough money to buy a bike. Flushed with pride, she coasted down the hill on her glamorous new "Victory bike" to deliver her papers in style. But the tires were narrow, rubber being scarce during the war. Pedaling those thin wheels up and down the long, unpaved back roads of her paper route was hard, painful work. Cruel reality soon dashed her dream. On aching legs, she walked the bike back up the hill to the barn and parked it. Next time, the papergirl swallowed her pride and put the bridle back on La Blue.

She completed first grade in the two-room schoolhouse in San Pedro where her mother taught. Then she was sent off to attend a larger school across the river, right next door to the Santa Cruz church. The new destination was a public school staffed by Dominican nuns. The sisters taught the lessons in English, demanded good and modest behavior, and administered periodic doses of castor oil. The dress code for girls required skirts with hems that fell four to five inches below the knee and beige cotton stockings that completely covered the legs.

Esther and her brother faced the same decision every morning when they headed off to school on their bikes. Should they ride the longer route down the road and across the bridge, or take the tempting shortcut straight across the river? The shortcut saved more than two miles, but the river was unpredictable. Some days, its flow was only a trickle. Other days, the flow was heavy and the current was strong.

One day the children pushed their luck and decided to take the shortcut, even though the flow was substantial. They took off their shoes and socks, tied their shoes together, and flung them around their necks to free their hands. Holding onto their bike seats with both hands, they waded in. Toward the middle of the river, where the current was strongest, Esther was swept off her feet. When she recovered her footing, her shoes were still around her neck but her stockings were gone.

When she got to school, she watched with chagrin as her teacher fulfilled the requirement for modesty. The resourceful nun covered the bare legs of the shivering girl with butcher paper, which she fastened with safety pins to the soggy hem of Esther's long skirt. "If those Sisters could see girls wearing miniskirts today, they'd turn over in their grave," Esther says ruefully. "How times have changed.

Trampas, NM. *Photo by John C. Collier, Jr., 1943. A homemaker in northern New Mexico mends clothing. In this community, the culture and economy had not changed significantly for several centuries. Courtesy New Mexico Museum of Art. New Mexico Farm Security Administration, museum purchase with funds from the Pinewood Foundation, with additional support from Barbara Erdman, 1990 (1990.70.278).*

CHAPTER 9
The Benefits of Change

Right up to the eve of World War II, colonial Spain's kingdom at the end of the earth had still experienced very little change in its culture and economy. The U.S. census of 1940 indicated that the most common occupation in the Española Valley was "farmer" or "farm laborer." Few residents had income-producing jobs. Most spoke Spanish at home, although their children attended schools where classes were taught in English.

The valley was on the threshold of change in 1942, as a fourth-grade tomboy was busy delivering newspapers and tagging along with her dad as he worked at his farm chores. She relished being outdoors but stayed inside one day while her mother was hosting a meeting of the Arte Antiguo club. Because Esther was good at drawing, Teofila had asked her to help the women "fix" one of their patterns — a deer with only three legs and indeterminate features.

The restored deer delighted her mother's friends, so Esther amused herself by enhancing other patterns for them. In the course of working with the club's stockpile of designs, she began imagining and drawing new versions of the old designs. Thrilled by her contributions, Teofila urged the young artist to continue creating new patterns for the women to copy and embroider.

The venerable colcha embroidery was her mother's passion, but Esther preferred making clothes for her doll on the old Singer treadle machine or sitting beside Teofila in the evening and working on some simple embroidery. As Esther continued to help the club with its designs, she also pursued other interests, conjuring up new adventures and exploring her world. An event in the fall of 1942 alerted her that that world was beginning to change.

Her father, Pedro, had an agreement with a man who owned a large apple orchard in Tesuque, a village just north of Santa Fe. Pedro agreed to work the man's land in exchange for half the harvest. Pedro's diligent work pruning, irrigating, weeding, and spraying the fruit trees during the year had produced a bumper crop. Esther was there, as usual, to help him. One morning during the harvest, a bus lumbered up the dusty lane to the orchard. The laborers who filed out of the bus were the strangest people she had ever seen — or heard. They spoke rapidly in a melodious language that sounded nothing at all like English or Spanish. The men were small and delicate. And they looked extremely happy, like children who had just been dropped off for a picnic.

The last man out of the bus wore a uniform and carried a rifle. Why on earth did this man bring a gun to an apple harvest? Esther pressed her father for answers. He told her simply that they were people he had hired.

The men spread out across the orchard and were soon delivering basketfuls of apples to the central collection point. During the afternoon, one of them discovered a wild herb growing along an irrigation ditch and shouted his finding to the others. They were excited. Esther couldn't understand their strange chatter, but it was obvious that they were delighted with their discovery.

Toting bags of apples and bunches of the wild herb they had been allowed to gather, the genteel men lined up at the end of the workday and bowed in gratitude to Pedro. Then the uniformed man with the rifle loaded the men back into the bus. Only later did Esther learn that those strange men were Japanese Americans from Camp Santa Fe, a twenty-eight-acre internment center a few miles down the road from the orchard.

After Japan attacked the U.S. naval base at Pearl Harbor in December 1941, the president of a nation gripped by fear ordered the FBI to pick up thousands of Japanese Americans living on the West Coast of the United States. Most were interned in ten large relocation centers. Those deemed the greatest threat to national security were shipped to secret facilities such as Camp Santa Fe and confined for the duration of the war. The men who spent the day harvesting Pedro's apple crop were teachers, ministers, Buddhist priests, bankers, store owners, and others who had held positions of influence in their communities. The first internees arrived in March 1942; the camp was closed in May 1946. During that time, some 4,550 men were incarcerated inside its barbed-wire fences.

As the Japanese Americans were harvesting Pedro's apple crop in the fall of 1942, Professor Robert Oppenheimer and General Leslie Groves were searching the mesas nearby for the ideal spot to establish a wartime laboratory where scientists could work in secrecy to develop an atomic weapon. The two men selected the site of the Los Alamos Ranch School, an elite prep school on the Pajarito Plateau less than twenty miles up the road from Camp Santa Fe. Groves noted in his autobiography that the site was the right place for the new laboratory because it was so well isolated and so far from "the ever-present threat of Japanese interference" (Groves 1962:65). Of course, Groves had no knowledge of the secret internment camp.

Although the rest of the world didn't learn about Oppenheimer's secret community on the Hill until the United States dropped the atomic bomb on Hiroshima and Nagasaki in 1945, Esther had the opportunity to experience life in Los Alamos firsthand. She had gone to live in Santa Fe with some close family friends, the Alvidres. She served as companion to their shy daughter and attended Loretto Academy as a day student. Mr. Alvidres, a skilled carpenter, was recruited to work on the project in Los Alamos. He asked the Lujans if they would allow Esther to remain with their daughter and move with the family to Los Alamos. The Lujans agreed, provided that she and the others were allowed to come and go from the town.

Esther had been to Los Alamos before. Pedro's brother-in-law Adolfo Montoya owned land and a home in Los Alamos and managed the gardens at the Los Alamos Ranch School. He had a knack for enriching the already rich volcanic soil of the plateau and raised all the flowers and vegetables for the school in extensive gardens near its main building, Fuller Lodge. In the 1930s, the Lujans had traveled the narrow, rutted, one-lane road that wound its way up the side of the Pajarito Plateau to visit Uncle Adolfo and his family. Esther remembered the pre–Manhattan Project Los Alamos as a place of beauty and serenity, where she had relaxed in the shade of tall pine trees and delighted in the sight of grassy mountain meadows filled with wildflowers.

When she arrived in Los Alamos with the Alvidres family, she was shocked to see how drastically the place had changed. The War Department had shut down the private boys' school, disbanded the faculty, and appropriated the school buildings for the technical personnel who came to work on the bomb project. She found herself in a crowded community that was bustling with activity and filled with new construction. Soldiers in formation paraded down muddy streets, trucks and jeeps raced by, and frowning men rushed past without as much as a nod.

Esther came to understand that her cup was half full, not half empty. Her new school offered impressive teachers, facilities, and activities. School supplies were plentiful. She had fascinating classmates, children of scientists from other nations who spoke with thick accents. And for physical education class during the winter months, the school took the students by bus to an ice-skating pond surrounded by beautiful pine trees.

Art classes exposed her to tools and techniques that nourished her innate talent and amplified her creativity. Academic classes that were not available in the valley helped her expand her understanding of the world. Greek mythology, it seemed, was simply the old Grimm's fairy tales reenacted in a new setting. Esther competed in spelling bees and worked especially hard for a demanding English teacher who was rumored to have been an army sergeant. That teacher helped her students understand the structure of the English language by making them diagram sentences.

One day a man came to their classroom and gave a lecture about the physics of the atom. He drew lots of circles on the blackboard and explained that a tremendous explosive reaction takes place when atoms split and collide with one another. The students had no idea what atoms were, or why he came to talk about them. Few people on the Hill, apart from the scientists themselves, knew the purpose of the project that was underway in that wartime community. Few had any idea that what they were doing in Los Alamos would change the world.

Well before it would change the world, the project on the Hill would change the valley's economy and lifestyle. Young people began to leave the farms to earn wages in nearby Los Alamos and in the wartime industries in other states. Change escalated as residents gained more training and more access to income-producing jobs. People in the valley's farming communities were beginning to emerge from the isolated world of their ancestors.

Esther's older sister Elizabeth had gone to California in 1940. She lived with a relative and studied to become a stenographer. She was hired by the government and sent to Japan to serve as a court reporter during war crime trials. Her income helped the family install plumbing in the old farmhouse in San Pedro. Brother Eddie also went to California, where he worked in his uncle's gas station and became a photographer. He bought a car. When he joined the air force and went off to war, he left the car in San Pedro.

Teofila applied for a position with the Atomic Energy Commission and in 1945 landed a job on the Hill. She used Eddie's car to commute to work. Her income enabled Pedro to buy the equipment he needed to make his farming efforts more productive and less labor intensive. Remaining true to her father's mandate that all his children receive an education, Teofila invested part of her paycheck in sending Esther back to Loretto Academy, the school Teofila had graduated from as a young woman so many years before.

Esther was a boarder at the respected school for young women for the balance of her high school years. After graduation, she was hired as a secretary at Los Alamos Scientific Laboratory. She earned enough to buy herself a car and install a butane tank for her parents to take the chill out of the rooms in the old farmhouse. With a new heating system, automobiles, and indoor plumbing, the family in San Pedro was, indeed, emerging from the past. The pace of life was accelerating, and changes were taking place — most of them for the good.

Although Esther didn't realize it at the time, it was the cumulative benefits of change that enabled her to move ever closer to her mature vision — to make the beloved embroidery of her mother and the Arte Antiguo into an art that would endure.

Colcha needle painting of the Christ Child of Atocha by Rebecca James. Created in 1960–1961 in Taos, New Mexico, the work is embroidery on linen with commercial wool yarn and metallic thread. Courtesy Museum of Spanish Colonial Art, Collections of the Spanish Colonial Arts Society, Inc., Santa Fe (1969.3).

CHAPTER 10

Anchoring the Thread: New Life for an Ancient Art

Rebecca James, an Englishwoman who came to New Mexico with artist Georgia O'Keeffe, experimented with colcha embroidery in the 1940s. Her work set the stage for the emergence of colcha as fine art. James learned the embroidery from Jesusita Perrault, a fellow resident of Taos. She studied the designs that Nellie Dunton had collected in the 1930s, reproduced the traditional work, then went on to create a series of original, embroidered pictures using the colcha stitch.

Frieda Lawrence, wife of novelist D. H. Lawrence, cited part of a letter she had received from James on needlework as a medium for artistic expression: "Talking about embroidery with you got me thinking about all the arts. In all of them, the hard thing to do is to transcend the tools and techniques. In painting you have a little stick with some hairs bound to it, a blob of color, and a blank surface to cover. . . . In embroidery it is a stiff little piece of shining steel and a thin thread. Certainly all small tools, but what an enormous expression they can make if the eye is true, the hands diligent, the mind disciplined, the spirit aware" (James 1963:18 – 19).

In 1963 the Museum of International Folk Art held an exhibition of James's imaginative needle paintings. But Esther — by this time a married woman living in Albuquerque and tending to the needs of a husband and three young children — was doubtless too busy to notice that colcha embroidery was on display in Santa Fe. Nor had she yet come to the conclusion that colcha embroidery could be thought of as art.

Esther had married José Aron Vigil in 1954 in the church of Santa Cruz, which both bride and groom had attended since birth. The newlyweds left for Albuquerque, where Joe had a job with the telephone company. Jeanette was born in 1957, Danny in 1960, Victor in 1961, and Stella in 1964.

Esther readily admits that she didn't even begin to understand and fully appreciate her Hispanic heritage until she had children of her own. She and Joe found great pleasure in telling them stories about their youth — the adventures they had, the people they knew and admired in their community, the food they ate, the celebrations they took part in. Slowly but surely, the proud parents instilled in their offspring a deep respect for their Hispanic culture and its history. They made frequent trips back to the valley to visit family and friends, attended services in the Santa Cruz church, and arranged for their city-bred children to spend time with their cousins and grandparents.

Teofila, by then a widow, was still living in the farmhouse in San Pedro. The Arte Antiguo was still going strong, and the Vigil family sometimes made the long drive to Española to join grandma at the club's annual picnic. In the summer of 1960, the event was held in Santa Clara Canyon and described in a newspaper clipping: "Sixty people enjoyed the picnic lunch and entertainment. Members, their families and guests were on hand for the fun despite a rain early in the afternoon. The menu consisted of roast beef, ham, sweet potatoes, beans and red chili, potato salad, green salad, cake, and coffee. Sopapillas were prepared at the picnic site."

In 1965 Joe was transferred to Santa Fe, where the family lived for the next five years. Esther worked part-time for the New Mexico State Legislative Council Service, and Teofila came to stay with baby Stella and the children while Esther was at work. An article from the late 1960s in the Española newspaper indicated that Teofila and three other members who had established the Arte Antiguo were still active participants. The women were still stitching diligently: "Members submit entries in the New Mexico State Fair each year and have had some of their work exhibited at the International Folk Art Museum in Santa Fe."

In 1968, the first year that Teofila exhibited her work at Spanish Market, she turned her sights on her daughter the artist. She managed to nudge Esther into joining her at the market. She was worried that her table was going to look empty; she needed more items to display and offer for sale. Esther had made a little blouse for Jeanette and embellished it with colcha designs. Teofila asked her to add that blouse to the display table: "You just take orders for the blouses, and I'll help you sew them." Busy raising four active youngsters, Esther was reluctant to get involved in a project concocted by her high-energy mother. But it was difficult to refuse her request for help. Esther set the price of a blouse at seventy-five dollars, hoping that few if any people would be willing to pay that much. To her dismay — and her mother's delight — many people did. It took Esther two years of hard work, and countless hours, to fill all the orders. After she had made a blouse and created a design (she hated to repeat herself, so she varied the designs), it took about sixty hours of embroidering to complete a single blouse.

Ever the activist, Teofila continued to exhibit her work at Spanish Market each summer and to promote colcha embroidery. Esther and her family encouraged Teofila, kept her company while she exhibited her work, and drove her to and from club meetings. But Esther, who figures she made less than one dollar an hour on the blouse project, had learned a hard lesson. She steered well clear of any more retail projects her mother might concoct.

The Arte Antiguo was still an active and esteemed organization in the Española community throughout the 1970s. Members served as grand marshals for the Oñate Fiesta parade in 1976 and held their customary *merienda* (tea) for dignitaries attending this fiesta. Then they celebrated the forty-second anniversary of the Arte Antiguo. "Club members have been reminiscing all this week," said an article in the *Rio Grande Sun*. "Mrs. Baca retrieved the ledger of minutes she has kept faithfully. From 1934, some members recall when the club sponsored a dance that cost as much as $26, $10.67 for the hall and $16 for the musicians."

In 1970 the Vigils moved back to Albuquerque, where Esther continued to focus on raising her children and instilling in them a respect for their heritage. She had enjoyed sewing clothes for herself since she took a class in home economics in seventh grade. She made dresses and blouses for herself and her daughters and, as time allowed, embellished the articles with colcha designs she created. One day her son Victor asked her to embroider some of those designs on a shirt for him. He was about eight years old and growing like a weed, so she was reluctant to comply with his request. She knew that a shirt she invested time in embroidering for him would get too small too soon.

Esther in northern New Mexico, gathering information about her mother's club. Photo by Nancy C. Benson.

But he persisted, so she went to the store and bought a shirt two sizes too large. When she finished embroidering the shirt, Victor rolled up the sleeves and wore it with pride. He finally did grow into that shirt. And then he continued to wear it and wear it. Eventually, he had to roll up the sleeves to disguise the fact that they were too short. Then it got too tight in the underarms. One day Esther heard him playing taps on his trumpet and assumed that one of the family pets had died. She was wrong. Victor was marking the official demise of his shirt. First the shirt had been too big for the boy; now the boy was too big for the shirt. He asked her to cut off the embroidery so he could save it and give it to his son someday.

In 1979 Joe and Esther celebrated their twenty-fifth wedding anniversary. By that time, Teofila could no longer manage to live alone in the old farmhouse in San Pedro and was living with them for much of the year. At a music-filled celebration in their backyard in Albuquerque, the children took turns dancing with the spry but aging grandmother who had always been such an important presence in their life.

That same year, Museum of New Mexico curator Alan Vedder asked the Arte Antiguo to embroider a special cloth for the main altar of the Santa Cruz church. In the course of restoration work on the altar screen of the historic church, Vedder and his team had discovered designs long hidden under layers of paint. Colcha embroidery motifs on the new altar cloth were to repeat and complement those designs. Teofila proudly volunteered to take on the project—an embroidery that would be nine feet long. But her eyesight had begun to deteriorate by the time Vedder's funding for the supplies finally came through.

Moved by her mother's plight, Esther assumed the responsibility of fulfilling the commitment Teofila had made. Her gesture heralded the commitment she would soon make to take up her mother's mantle and devote herself to preserving the ancient art. She told Teofila not to worry, took a deep breath, and threw herself into the project—a huge amount of embroidering that took her several months to complete. She had to work on it all day and sometimes continued stitching until two in the morning.

When she completed her labor of love and delivered it to the church in 1983, she was repeating an act of devotion made on the same spot two hundred years before. One of the earliest records of colcha embroidery is a listing in the Santa Cruz church inventory of "a new colcha that serves as the carpet for the high altar which was given by a pious woman" in 1782. Esther was also being drawn ever more deeply into her mother's beloved needlework.

Even though Teofila had lost most of her eyesight, she continued her dedication to the Arte Antiguo and its efforts to preserve the colcha embroidery tradition. A photo in the *Rio Grande Sun* shows seven members attending a celebration of the club's fiftieth anniversary in 1984. Four of the seven women were among its earliest members: Teofila, Aggie Serna, Flora Roybal, and Eloisa Maestas. Teofila, ninety-one years old and practically blind, still manages a smile for the photographer. She is wearing a blouse decorated with colcha embroidery.

She died in 1995, and the Arte Antiguo expired that same year. Once all the charter members were gone, it was hard to recruit new members to carry on the work. Tillie Gonzales, one of only three remaining members, regretfully participated in the vote to close the checking account and disband the club. Its commitment to preserving colcha embroidery had lasted for more than sixty years.

Tillie Gonzalez shares her embroidery and her memories of the Arte Antiguo with Esther. The large tablecloth Tillie made for her dining room includes the popular motif from Curtin collection "colcha no. 3" in the 1935 instruction booklet (see page 124). Photo by Nancy C. Benson.

Opposite: Colcha wall hanging by Esther Vigil, 14.5 by 26 inches, wool embroidery on sabanilla and on a cotton border. The lower portion of the design is solid embroidery; the top portion is stand-alone figures. Photo by Dan Richey. Courtesy of Nancy C. Benson.

It was only after Teofila and the Arte Antiguo were gone that Esther realized how much she had taken the embroidery for granted. Colcha had always been present in her life. She understood how important it had been to her mother and the club and resolved that their efforts would not be forgotten. She determined to place images of the beautiful work squarely in the foreground of other people's lives.

Esther arrived at the understanding that she could deploy her innate talent in art and design to keep colcha alive by creating exciting new textures, color schemes, and compositions in the embroidery. The girl who had sketched patterns for the Arte Antiguo would bring new life to colcha. She would transcend the techniques and traditional patterns preserved in the instruction booklet produced by the New Mexico Department of Vocational Education and Training in 1935. She would work to secure the fragile thread of the colcha tradition by elevating the embroidery of her ancestors from a folk art to a fine art.

She began her campaign with her immediate family. She made sure that the images of colcha were part of the daily lives of her children and grandchildren. Her designs, reproduced with a paintbrush, flow over the arched entry in Jeanette's house. Lights glow softly through the colcha patterns she punched in sheets of copper to highlight the *nichos* (alcoves) in Victor's home. Framed examples of her embroidery are spotlighted in the homes of all four children. And beside their beds, all her grandchildren have distinctive colcha angels that watch over them and remind them of their heritage.

In 2001 Esther broadened her campaign to make the world aware of the art of colcha embroidery. She began doing demonstrations of the embroidery at a market center south of Santa Fe that promotes the traditional arts and crafts of New Mexico. The first year, few visitors knew what she was doing. Their lack of awareness of the embroidery tradition only firmed her resolve.

She returned to her demonstrations the following summer with several dramatic new embroideries displayed in traditional tin frames that she had punched with colcha designs. Interest grew. Visitors asked lots of questions and remarked on the beauty of her work. The next year, the *Albuquerque Journal* interviewed her and ran a full-color, full-page spread of her needlework. The article appeared on the Sunday of her demonstration at the market center. When she arrived, there was standing room only.

Two dozen people in the crowd wrote down their contact information and asked Esther if she would be willing to teach them how to do the embroidery. Since then, she has developed and taught a series of classes. She takes pride in the fact that her students come from all walks of life and from many

Top: Wool-on-cotton colcha by Esther Vigil, solid embroidery, 21 by 28 inches framed. Esther designed and punched the tin frame with motifs that echo those of the embroidery. Photo by Tony Reynolds. Courtesy of Esther Vigil.

Bottom: Wool-on-cotton colcha by Esther Vigil, solid embroidery, 22 by 25 inches framed. Esther designed and constructed the tin frame. Photo by Tony Reynolds. Courtesy of Esther Vigil.

different cultures. In 2006 she wrote, illustrated, and published *Colcha* — an instruction manual for her students.

The manual includes information on the history and technique of the embroidery, as well as fifteen new patterns she created that are based on traditional designs. In the preface to the manual, she makes an unequivocal statement: "I've written this for only one reason: to preserve the Spanish colonial art of colcha embroidery by getting others as addicted to it as I am."

In March 2004, the Albuquerque Museum invited her to do a demonstration in conjunction with its exhibition of colcha embroidery. One of the works on exhibit was a large bedspread that her mother had made in 1977. The bedspread contains seventy-two stand-alone figures, and Esther remembered that she had created many of those figures from her own imagination when Teofila discovered she didn't have enough to fill such a large area. As she sat alongside the display of her mother's embroidery and worked on her own, Esther smiled as she reflected on how Teofila had drawn her into the ancient art.

Gaining momentum in her quest to anchor the tenuous thread of colcha embroidery for future generations, Esther has become increasingly confident in her ability to create new works of art. To celebrate

Wool-on-cotton colcha (and reverse side) by Esther Vigil. A photo of the colcha appears as the front cover of her instruction manual. Photos by Dan Richey. Courtesy of Esther Vigil.

their fiftieth wedding anniversary in 2004, she designed and produced an innovative tribute to her and Joe's Hispanic heritage — a Sagrada Familia that combines the traditional techniques of embroidery and tinwork. She drew and embroidered what Rebecca James would have called a needle painting of the three figures of the Holy Family and designed for it a carrying case of tin that she punched with colcha patterns.

She speaks of this new work as a dream to represent part of her past and inspire continuing devotion in her children and their families. The work embodies her vivid memories of the beautiful capillita of the Holy Family that arrived at the old farmhouse every month. The candles that Teofila lit. The prayers they all said together in the evening.

For Teofila's funeral mass in the Santa Cruz church, the altar was lined with Sagrada Familias, including the one the Lujans received in their home for so many years. Esther took her new capillita to that venerable old church to be blessed during a special service honoring the life of Father Manyanet, founder of the Holy Family

Above: One of fifteen new colcha embroidery patterns included in Esther's instruction manual. Courtesy of Esther Vigil.

Left: Wool-on-cotton colcha by Esther Vigil, solid embroidery, 11 by 13 inches. The pattern for the embroidery is provided in her instruction manual. Photo by Tony Reynolds. Courtesy of Esther Vigil.

Above: Wool-on-wool, solid embroidery colcha by Esther Vigil, 24.5 by 40.5 inches. Photo by Tony Reynolds. Courtesy of Esther Vigil.

Right: Details of the central motif and reverse side of colcha. Photos by Tony Reynolds.

tradition. When Esther and Joe renewed their wedding vows in a private chapel in Albuquerque, the new work of art held a place of honor during the ceremony. It sat atop the altar cloth that Esther had embroidered on behalf of Teofila for the church where their families had worshipped for so many years.

At the end of the ceremony, their grandchildren reverently closed the capillita and carried the new heirloom to a reception hall nearby, where family and friends dined on good food and danced to the lively beat of mariachis. It was a gala that Teofila and the women of the Arte Antigua would surely have relished. Their decades of effort had borne fruit. The ancient art of colcha embroidery will bring joy to future generations.

Top: The Sagrada Familia that Esther made to mark the fiftieth anniversary of her marriage to Joe. Photo by Tony Reynolds. Courtesy of Esther Vigil.

Bottom: Wool-on-cotton colcha by Esther Vigil, solid embroidery, 9 by 16.5 inches. The dark green background colcha stitches are under completion. Photo by Tony Reynolds. Courtesy of Esther Vigil.

REFERENCES

Ahlborn, Richard. 1983. Frontier Possessions: The Evidence from Colonial Documents. In *Colonial Frontiers: Art and Life in Spanish New Mexico, The Fred Harvey Collection*, ed. Christine Mather. Pp. 35 – 44. Santa Fe, NM: Ancient City Press.

Applegate, Frank, and Mary Austin. N.d. Spanish Colonial Arts. Unpublished manuscript. T. M. Pearce papers in the University of New Mexico Center for Southwest Research. MSS 255 BC, box 2, folder 20.

Benson, Nancy. 1980. Preserving an Early Hispanic Art. *Empire Magazine*. June 8.

Boyd, E. 1974. *Popular Arts of Spanish New Mexico*. Santa Fe: Museum of New Mexico Press.

Boyle, Susan. 1997. *Los Capitalistas: Hispano Merchants and the Santa Fe Trade*. Albuquerque: University of New Mexico Press.

Burke, James. 1973. *This Miserable Kingdom*. Albuquerque, NM: Our Lady of Fatima Church.

Cash, Marie Romero. 1993. *Built of Earth and Song: Churches of Northern New Mexico*. Santa Fe, NM: Red Crane Books.

Cirillo, Dexter. 1998. *Across Frontiers: Hispanic Crafts of New Mexico*. San Francisco: Chronicle Books.

Curiel, Gustavo. 1999. *Pintura y Vida Cotidiana en Mexico, 1650–1950*. Mexico City: Fomento Cultural Banamex.

deBuys, William. 1985. *Enchantment and Exploitation: The Life and Hard Times of a New Mexico Mountain Range*. Albuquerque: University of New Mexico Press.

Dickey, Roland. 1949. *New Mexico Village Arts*. Albuquerque: University of New Mexico Press.

Dunton, Nellie. 1935. *The Spanish Colonial Ornament and the Motifs Depicted in the Textiles of the Period of the American Southwest*. Philadelphia: H. C. Perleberg.

Ellis, Florence Hawley. 1989. *San Gabriel del Yungue: As Seen by an Archaeologist*. Santa Fe, NM: Sunstone Press.

Ellis, Susan. 1980. *New Mexico Colcha Embroidery*. Albuquerque, NM: Susan H. Ellis.

Emery, Irene. 1949. Wool Embroideries of New Mexico: Some Notes on the Stitch Employed. *El Palacio* 56(11):339 – 45.

———. 1950. Wool Embroideries of New Mexico: Notes on Some of the Spanish Terms. *El Palacio* 57(5):142 – 52.

Espinosa, Carmen. 1935. *New Mexico Colonial Embroidery*. Santa Fe: New Mexico Department of Vocational Education and Training.

Esquibel, José Antonio. 1994. Doña Eufemia, La Valerosa: The Great Martesia of Oñate's Colony. *Herencia* 2(2):19 – 28.

Fisher, Nora, ed. 1979. *Spanish Textile Tradition of New Mexico and Colorado*. Santa Fe: Museum of New Mexico Press.

Garcia, David. 2007. Digging in the Dirt: Archaeologists Share What Lay Beneath Sweeney Center. *Santa Fe Reporter*. May 16 – 22.

Gavin, Robin Farwell. 1994. *Traditional Arts of Spanish New Mexico: The Hispanic Heritage Wing at the Museum of International Folk Art*. Santa Fe: Museum of New Mexico Press.

Groves, Leslie. 1962. *Now It Can Be Told: The Story of the Manhattan Project*. New York: Harper.

Hackett, Charles, ed. 1923. *Historical Documents Relating to New Mexico, Nueva Vizcaya, and Approaches Thereto, to 1773*. Vols. 1 and 2. Washington, DC: Carnegie Institution of Washington.

Harris, Jennifer, ed. 1993. *Five Thousand Years of Textiles*. Washington, DC: Smithsonian Books in association with the British Museum Press.

Haufmann, Rita. 2007. Rita Padilla Haufmann, Spinner-Dyer-Weaver. Information sheet. Tesuque, NM: Rita Padilla Haufmann.

James, Rebecca. 1963. *The Colcha Stitch: Embroideries by Rebecca James*. Santa Fe, NM: Museum of International Folk Art.

Jenkins, Myra Ellen. 1983. Some Eighteenth-Century New Mexico Women of Property. In *Hispanic Arts and Ethnohistory in the Southwest*, ed. Marta Weigle. Pp. 335 – 45. Santa Fe, NM: Ancient City Press.

Jones, Oakah L., Jr. 1979. *Los Paisanos: Spanish Settlers on the Northern Frontier of New Spain*. Norman: University of Oklahoma Press.

Katzew, Ilona. 2004. *Casta Painting: Images of Race in Eighteenth-Century Mexico*. New Haven, CT: Yale University Press.

Kessell, John. 2002. *Spain in the Southwest: A Narrative History of Colonial New Mexico, Arizona, Texas, and California*. Norman: University of Oklahoma Press.

———. 2004. Not That Remote: Diego de Vargas and His Household in Santa Fe. *El Palacio* 109(1):27 – 30.

Kessell, John, Rick Hendricks, Meredith Dodge, and Larry Miller, eds. 2002. *A Settling of Accounts: The Journals of don Diego de Vargas, New Mexico, 1700 – 1704.* Albuquerque: University of New Mexico Press.

Lambert, Marjorie. 1953. The Oldest Armor Found in the United States: The San Gabriel del Yunque Helmet. *Archaeology* 6(2):108 – 10.

MacAulay, Suzanne. 2000. *Stitching Rites: Colcha Embroidery along the Northern Rio Grande.* Tucson: University of Arizona Press.

Mexican Archives of New Mexico. New Mexico State Records Center and Archives, Santa Fe.

Minge, Ward Alan. 1979. Efectos del País: A History of Weaving along the Rio Grande. In *Spanish Textile Tradition of New Mexico and Colorado,* ed. Nora Fisher. Pp. 8 – 28. Santa Fe: Museum of New Mexico Press.

Montaño, Mary. 2001. *Tradiciones Nuevomexicanas: Hispano Arts and Culture of New Mexico.* Albuquerque: University of New Mexico Press.

Morgan, Beth. 1987. Sewing Circle with a Difference. *Rio Grande Sun.* October 1.

Nestor, Sarah. 1978. *The Native Market of the Spanish New Mexican Craftsmen: Santa Fe, 1933–1940.* Santa Fe: Colonial New Mexico Historical Foundation.

Nunn, Tey Marianna. 2001. *Sin Nombre: Hispana and Hispano Artists of the New Deal Era.* Albuquerque: University of New Mexico Press.

Oettinger, Marion, Jr., ed. 1997. *Folk Art of Spain and the Americas: El Alma del Pueblo.* San Antonio, TX: San Antonio Museum of Art.

Padilla, Carmella, ed. 2002. *Conexiones: Connections in Spanish Colonial Art.* Santa Fe, NM: Museum of Spanish Colonial Art.

Palmer, Gabrielle, and Donna Pierce. 1992. *Cambios: The Spirit of Transformation in Spanish Colonial Art*. Albuquerque: Santa Barbara Museum of Art in cooperation with University of New Mexico Press.

Pelauzy, Maria Antonia. 1978. *Spanish Folk Crafts,* trans. Diorki. Barcelona: Editorial Blume.

———. 1997. Common Themes and Regional Variations. In *Folk Art of Spain and the Americas: El Alma del Pueblo,* ed. Marion Oettinger, Jr. Pp. 31 – 35. San Antonio, TX: San Antonio Museum of Art.

Pierce, Donna, and Marta Weigle, eds. 1996. *Spanish New Mexico: The Collections of the Spanish Colonial Arts Society*. Santa Fe: Museum of New Mexico Press.

Pinel, Carlos. 1997. Popular Furniture. In *Folk Art of Spain and the Americas: El Alma del Pueblo,* ed. Marion Oettinger, Jr. Pp. 81-93. San Antonio, TX: San Antonio Museum of Art.

Post, Stephen. 2006. Buildings Lost and Found: Eighteenth-Century Foundations of a New Museum. *El Palacio* 3(4):38 – 41, 90.

Ricard, Robert. 1966. *The Spiritual Conquest of Mexico,* trans. Lesley B. Simpson. Berkeley: University of California Press.

Roberts, Calvin, and Susan Roberts. 1946. *New Mexico*. Albuquerque: University of New Mexico Press.

Roberts, David. 2004. *The Pueblo Revolt: The Secret Rebellion That Drove the Spaniards Out of the Southwest*. New York: Simon and Schuster.

Sagel, Jim, ed. 1983. *La Iglesia de Santa Cruz de la Cañada*. Santa Cruz, NM: Santa Cruz Parish.

Scholes, France. 1937. Troublous Times in New Mexico 1659 – 1670. Chapter III: The Administration of López. *New Mexico Historical Review* 12(4):380 – 91.

Slaney, Deborah. 2005. *Wonders of the Weavers: Nineteenth-Century Rio Grande Weavings from the Collection of the Albuquerque Museum*. Albuquerque, NM: Albuquerque Museum.

Simmons, Marc. 1988. *New Mexico: An Interpretive History*. Albuquerque: University of New Mexico Press.

———. 1991. *Coronado's Land: Essays on Daily Life in Colonial New Mexico*. Albuquerque: University of New Mexico Press.

———. 2001. *Spanish Pathways: Readings in the History of Hispanic New Mexico*. Albuquerque: University of New Mexico Press.

Sinclair, John. 1951. San Gabriel de Yunque Yunque. *American Heritage* 2(2):8–11, 62.

Spanish Archives of New Mexico, Series 1. New Mexico State Records Center, Santa Fe.

Spanish Archives of New Mexico, Series 2. New Mexico State Records Center, Santa Fe.

Staniland, Kay. 1991. *Medieval Craftsmen: Embroiderers*. London: British Museum Press.

Stoller, Marianne. 1977. Traditional Hispanic Arts and Crafts in the San Luis Valley of Colorado. In *Hispanic Crafts of the Southwest*, ed. William Wroth. Pp. 81 – 96. Colorado Springs, CO: Taylor Museum of the Colorado Springs Fine Arts Center.

———. 1979. Spanish-Americans, Their Servants and Sheep: A Culture History of Weaving in Southern Colorado. In *Spanish Textile Tradition of New Mexico and Colorado*, ed. Nora Fisher. Pp. 37–52. Santa Fe: Museum of New Mexico Press.

Taylor, Lonn, and Dessa Bokides. 1987. *New Mexican Furniture, 1600 – 1940: The Origins, Survival, and Revival of Furniture Making in the Hispanic Southwest*. Santa Fe: Museum of New Mexico Press.

Thorp, Annette Hesch. 1941. Vicenta. Federal Writers' Project Manuscripts. Museum of New Mexico History Library. MNM 5-5-53 number 1. May 6, May 13.

Torrez, Robert. 2005. Spanish/Indian Relations in Colonial New Mexico. Lecture presented at the Institute for Lifelong Learning, Albuquerque. March 17.

Toussaint, Manuel. 1967. *Colonial Art in Mexico,* trans. and ed. Elizabeth W. Weismann. Austin: University of Texas Press.

Usner, Don. 1995. *Sabino's Map: Life in Chimayó's Old Plaza.* Santa Fe: Museum of New Mexico Press.

Vigil, Esther. 2006. *Colcha.* Albuquerque, NM: Esther Vigil.

Villagrá, Gaspar Pérez de. [1610] 1992. *Historia de la Nueva México,* trans. and ed. Miguel Encinias, Alfred Rodriguez, and Joseph P. Sanchez. Albuquerque: University of New Mexico Press.

Weigle, Marta, ed. 1975. *Hispanic Villages of Northern New Mexico.* Santa Fe, NM: Lightning Tree.

———, ed. 1983. *Hispanic Arts and Ethnohistory in the Southwest: New Papers Inspired by the Work of E. Boyd.* Santa Fe, NM: Ancient City Press.

Wheat, Joe Ben. 2003. *Blanket Weaving in the Southwest,* ed. Ann Hedlund. Tucson: University of Arizona Press.

Wheelwright, Mary Cabot. 1932. Some Embroideries from New Mexico. *Bulletin of the Needle and Bobbin Club* 16(2):19 – 27.

Whitaker, Robert. 2004. *The Mapmaker's Wife.* New York: Bantam Dell.

Wirth, John, and Linda Harvey Aldrich. 2003. *Los Alamos: The Ranch School Years, 1917–1943.* Albuquerque: University of New Mexico Press.

Wroth, William, ed. 1977. *Hispanic Crafts of the Southwest.* Colorado Springs, CO: Taylor Museum of the Colorado Springs Fine Arts Center.

INDEX